CROSS-SELLING SUCCESS

Also by Ford Harding

Rain Making: The Professional's Guide
to Attracting New Clients

Creating Rainmakers: The Manager's Guide to Training
Professionals to Attract New Clients

CROSS-SELLING SUCCESS

A Rainmaker's Guide to Professional Account Development

FORD HARDING

Adams Media Corporation
Avon, Massachusetts

Copyright ©2002 Ford Harding. All rights reserved. This book, or parts thereof, may not be reproduced in any form without permission from the publisher; exceptions are made for brief excerpts used in published reviews.

Published by Adams Media Corporation
57 Littlefield Street, Avon, MA 02322. U.S.A.
www.adamsmedia.com

ISBN: 1-58062-705-6

Printed in Canada.

J I H G F E D C B A

Library of Congress Cataloging-in-Publication Data
available from the publisher.

BEST Selling® is a service mark owned exclusively by Charles Ford Harding, and has been filed with the United States Patent and Trademark Office. For the sake of convenience, full service mark notice is not reiterated for each use of BEST Selling service mark within the text. However, all rights in the BEST Selling service mark are exclusively reserved.

This publication is designed to provide accurate and authoritative information with regard to the subject matter covered. It is sold with the understanding that the publisher is not engaged in rendering legal, accounting, or other professional advice. If legal advice or other expert assistance is required, the services of a competent professional person should be sought.

— From a *Declaration of Principles* jointly adopted by a
Committee of the American Bar Association
and a Committee of Publishers and Associations

This book is available for quantity discounts for bulk purchases.
For information call 1-800-872-5627.

Visit our home page at *www.adamsmedia.com*

Contents

Acknowledgments vii

Introduction: Why Cross Sell? xi

Part I: The BEST Selling Model for Cross-Selling Success. 1

1. What Is Cross Selling? 3

2. How Rainmakers Do It: An Overview of the BEST Selling Model 15

3. Portal Projects: Getting in the Door 23

4. Buyers: The People We Need to Know 41

5. Events: How You Drive the Process 55

6. Signals: How We Know a Client May Need More Services 73

7. Techniques: Tools for Making It Happen 89

8. Summary: Bringing the Parts Together 109

Part II: BEST Selling Within the Context of the Firm.................**117**

9. Allocating Resources to Accounts.............119

10. Professionals and Salespeople: Mix Well Before Serving (With John Mirro)..................133

11. Rules of Engagement.......................145

12. Overcoming Functional Thinking: Cross Selling and Communications (With Dallas Kersey) 157

13. Rewarding Cross Selling (With Alan Johnson) ..179

14. Cross-Selling Failures 191

15. Ethics and Cross Selling 205

16. Conclusion...............................217

Notes 219

Index..225

Acknowledgments

This book is based on research and most of that research consists of interviews with professionals who are successful at cross selling services. I greatly appreciate all the time these people took and their willingness to share openly both good cross-selling experiences as well as bad ones. This book is built around stories, the experiences of these people told in their own words. Truth is more interesting and educational than fiction. Their stories are more valuable than anything I could have made up or drawn from my own, more limited experience.

Among the accountants, architects, consulting engineers, executive recruiters, industrial designers, lawyers, and management consultants who gave their time are Will Archie, Carol Benjamin, Bruce Beverly, Bob Borsch, Jeff Boudreau, Neil Burger, Joe Buskuhl, Abby Gouverneur Carr, Joe Caso, Gary Cawthorne, Hollace Cohen, Jim Corey, Mike Corey, Henrik Danholt, Dwight Davies, Gene Delves, Audie Dunham, Rich Finkelstein, Bill Fredericks, Dave Fritz, Guy Geier, Bill Gustafson, David Harris, Wayne Hauge, Bob Hirth, Wayne Hoeberlein, Martin Hoenle, Anita Hotchkiss, Frank Jacoby, Jack Jolls, Ed Kasparek, Dave Keyko, Bob Krauss, Paul Kohlenbrener, Bill Lee, Carl LoBue, Rocco Maggiotto, Ray Manganelli, Chris Maynard, Bob McKee,

Dan Meiland, Tom Murnane, Lauren McCracken, Grady Means, David Nash, Terry Noetzel, Connie O'Hare, Dave Osterman, Mike Palmer, Mike Peters, Stan Phernambucq, Whitney Pidot, Gary Pines, Dave Ping, Pat Pollino, Roger Pratesi, Bob Prieto, Steve Quinn, Roy Riedlinger, Muriel Robinette, Frank Ruotolo, Jim Schriner, Barry Seymour, Beth Sher, Les Sherman, Bill Shine, Milt Smith, Dennis Sullivan, Bruce Tindale, Steve Vernon, Mark Weitzel, Alan Weyl, Ian B. Wilson, and Emad Youssef. Several people I interviewed prefer to remain anonymous. I appreciate their help, too.

Many people provided introductions to the professionals whom I interviewed. Without those introductions this book would not have been possible. Among those who helped in this way are John Bliss, Neil Burger, Abby Gouverneur Carr, Jeanne Caswell, George Friedel, Carol Greenwald, Derek HasBrouck, David Haygood, Dallas Kersey, Ron Madden, John Miniutti, Cheryl Ovary, Mike Peters, Ed Scheuer, Les Sherman, Elizabeth Sosnow, Mimi Spangler, Bobbi Stroupe, Tim Travers, and Mike Ulekowski.

Many of the concepts presented in this book were developed during work for clients. Like all professionals, I am deeply indebted to these clients for their support and the stimulation that came from working with them.

Several people provided insights into issues I was struggling with. Thanks to Mary Stone, Clay Crpek, and Bill Miner for bettering my understanding of the cost of switching actuaries. George Davis provided helpful insights into the ways professionals are used in mergers and acquisitions, based on frontline experience. Gene Delves gave a lively description of the history of cross selling at Arthur Andersen, now known simply as Andersen, one of the first professional firms to focus on the issue, long before its recent hard times. The section on solution sets owes much to conversations with Jim Corey, Henrik Danholt, Ray Manganelli, Bruce

Tindale, and Ian B. Wilson. That three of these people are Europeans suggests that this is an area in which those of us in the United States may have some catching up to do. Mike Peters made available his experiences on getting professionals and salespeople to work together.

Laurie Young and Dallas Kersey reviewed the chapter on rules of engagement and provided extremely helpful insights, based on their experiences with large organizations.

Three people helped write chapters where I felt the need for specialized knowledge. John Mirro of Sybase co-authored Chapter 10 on getting professionals and salespeople to work together. That chapter originally appeared in *C2M* and is reprinted here with permission in slightly modified form. Dallas Kersey of Kersey Strategic Communications wrote much of Chapter 12 on communications, and Alan Johnson of Johnson & Associates wrote most of Chapter 13 on rewarding cross selling.

Many thanks to my agent, Jeff Herman, for shepherding this book through acceptance and to Claire Gerus for her editing and suggestions. Anita Dennis reviewed the final draft for errors. This book is better for their help.

All of these people are responsible for much of the good that can be found in this book. I am responsible for the bad.

I want to thank my wife, Liz, and son, Charles, for the patience they had with this project, which occupied many hours that might better have been spent with them. This book is dedicated to Dinny Greene, Judy Harding, and Jon Harding for all the support and love they have given over the years. Nothing is more important than family.

Introduction: Why Cross Sell?

"We have been working with [a metal fabricator] for over a year. Yesterday, I learned that [another consulting firm] has just sold a major project there that we could have done. We didn't get a chance to bid on it. We didn't even know the client was looking for the service. It drives me crazy." So spoke the managing partner of a management consulting firm, describing an experience all too frequent at professional firms and other companies.

On another occasion, the managing partner of an accounting firm told me this story:

> We have a large client in Washington, D.C., whom I went to visit when I was in town a while ago. The partner who managed the account told me, "The CEO is my good buddy. I go golfing with this guy." I met with several people at the client's, two of them in the information technology area, just to talk about all of the things we do. Both of the people in the technology area said, "I didn't know you did that. When I needed that service recently, I hired somebody else." All the discussions they had had with our people centered around the audit work we were doing, instead of the work we could have been doing. Our partner had

even gone golfing with the CEO and not talked about our other services!

These problems happen in all kinds of firms, as this story about a mess-up at a full-service consulting engineering firm shows:

> Our Connecticut office was doing some mechanical and electrical office fit up work for a drug manufacturer. One day a member of the structural department in our New York office told me that his department had just won a project to help design a new 250,000-square-foot headquarters for the same company. He hadn't known that our Connecticut office was working for the client, and the people in the Connecticut office hadn't known about the new headquarters project.
>
> This was a double failure. Because of our existing relationship, we probably could have gotten the mechanical and electrical work for the whole headquarters if we hadn't slipped up.

There are lots of stories like these. Management at most firms recognizes the huge potential benefits from selling more services to existing clients. But failures to do so are common, sometimes for pitiful reasons.

We frequently ask the professionals we work with how much their revenues would increase if all the people in their firms simply recognized opportunities for additional services and passed that information on to the partners heading up the accounts. Some say they would have all the work they could handle. In fact, we have never heard back a figure of less than 10 percent. Think of it—10 percent increase in revenues simply from people listening better and passing information on to those in charge of accounts!

Of course, the benefits can be even greater if a firm really works at cross selling and succeeds at it. The most commonly cited benefits are:

More value to our clients. Ultimately, professionals are judged on the value they provide their clients. Large projects that require integrating several services usually provide more value than small ones. The late Milton Stern, a tax, trust, and estate attorney in New Jersey, helped build what was at the time the largest law firm in the state because he realized that his small-business clients had needs beyond simple tax and estate problems. These issues were intermingled with their other family and business issues. By offering his clients the full range of his firm's services, he was able to provide them much greater value and also helped grow his firm.

Some clients see so much value in being able to buy a wide range of services from a professional that they will shun firms offering a narrower range. Bob Krauss was a partner at a mid-sized Philadelphia law firm that merged with a larger firm, Schnader Harrison Segal & Lewis. After the merger, he found that he was able to win back several clients who had chosen not to work with him at the smaller firm. "They had liked our corporate capability but needed a firm with intellectual capital capability, too."

Increased profit. Often, the larger an account, the more profitable it is. Firms increase their efficiency by providing multiple services to the same client because they know what the client needs and how the client operates. Often, selling costs are reduced if the work is sole-sourced, or the process used to hire a professional is simplified, as is often the case for cross-sold projects.

For example, an interior design firm that designs several regional customer service offices for a client sees all of these benefits. Its selling costs drop and it can design the third or fourth center much more efficiently than the first. Its people learn a lot about the client's objectives, facilities standards, and program requirements from work done on the early projects.

More loyal clients. Clients who receive several services tend to be more loyal than those who receive a single service. It becomes harder for the client to totally sever the relationship, should something go wrong. The multiple relationships and values you are providing can help you buy time while you fix the problem. If business in one area drops off, the firm is often able to hang onto business in another. In time, professionals may be able to rebuild the relationship from this alternate position, a task that would be much more difficult if they were no longer working with the client.

For example, two partners in the retirement practice of a benefits and compensation consulting firm left the firm to establish their own company. When they left, they took with them the retirement business of a large telecommunications company. However, their former employer still had a foothold by providing the client with several other services. Through judicious account management, the firm has rebuilt the relationship, so that it is producing more fees than it had before losing the retirement business. They are now well positioned to win back the retirement business, should the departed partners ever stumble.

Selling multiple services can also help you when someone in your firm makes a mistake. A law firm was hired to represent a large pharmaceuticals company involved in a race discrimination case. A community activist had been leading demonstrations in front of the company's headquarters, and top management wanted the issue resolved. The lawyers analyzed the situation and found one legitimate discrimination case, which they recommended the client settle. They then proceeded to negotiate good severance packages for other plaintiffs who wanted to leave, and helped ease the way for still others who wanted to return to their jobs. Three cases went to court, which the client won. The general counsel was exceedingly grateful for the variety of services the law firm provided.

However, another associate of the same firm was working on another legal matter. She became upset with one of the client's in-house counsel and had a heated argument with him at a meeting at which several other people from the client's office were present. The in-house counsel was embarrassed and angry. After this, the firm was only able to retain the account because of the strong relationships it had formed with the general counsel's office by handling the discrimination cases with such positive results.

Working in several areas with a client has another benefit: it improves your knowledge and understanding of the company's issues. This, in turn, allows you to provide better service. One consultant knew many people in many departments at a huge communications company because he had participated in a variety of projects there. He would call these people from time to time to see how they were doing, and learn what problems they were facing. From these conversations, he was sometimes able to piece together a picture of an issue the company was facing that those internally hadn't focused on. When that happened he would send off a letter to the president, also a friend, describing the issue and suggesting that they talk. "Four out of five times, I would get a note back saying that they had the issue covered, but about every fifth time I would get a call from his secretary to schedule a meeting. Those meetings usually resulted in big projects."

If you work in a variety of areas in a company, you know—and are known by—more people there. That can be of tremendous value when your position in the account is threatened for any reason. This point was brought home in a story from Carl LoBue, founder of the consulting firm LoBue Associates:

We were doing some work in Florida for [a bank]. It had been a long-term client that we had worked for all over the world. Just as this project started, the CEO of the unit was transfered to another business. In a lot of cases that can cost a consultant the project. In this case, the guy who replaced him was someone we had worked for in the Pacific. Because of that we didn't miss a beat on the work. He was comfortable continuing the project.

The more people you know in an account, the greater your chances of hearing about new opportunities as they arise. In this way success feeds success. The more work you do, the more work you are likely to get.

The ability to grow when selling to an industry that is consolidating. Banking, insurance, electric power, telecommunications, and many other industries are consolidating. This means there will be fewer, larger clients to sell to in these industries. Competition for these accounts will of course increase as a result. Cross selling is one way to continue to grow in such markets.

When two large organizations merge, each brings along with it a set of professionals: an auditor, an actuary, a labor and employment attorney, and so on. Often, by the time the merger is completed, only one professional of each type survives—usually from the firm that represents the dominant company in the merger. However, a firm that sells many services to an account is far more likely to survive a merger than one that provides a single service.

At the same time, the firm that loses out in a merger must make up the lost billings elsewhere, and one solution is to sell more work to its other clients.

The ability to grow in mature markets. Growth in mature markets is painful because it must come at the expense of entrenched competitors. For example, all large financial institutions already have an auditor. Therefore, an accounting firm wishing to grow its audit practice in this industry will have to steal business from its competitors, an expensive and time-consuming undertaking. That same firm may continue growing more easily by selling additional services to its present clients. One professional firm we know has been so successful, it is now doing business with 90 percent of the companies in its market. Selling different kinds of work to the clients it already has is the primary way that it has left to continue growing.

The ability to add practices. A firm can often grow new practices rapidly by selling its services to existing accounts. Frank Jacoby, an accountant and consultant, has started many new practices over his career. He says, "During the first year of a new practice, up to 90 percent of the business may come from the core business. Later, that isn't true." Many of the rainmakers we interviewed for this book alluded to this benefit of cross selling.

When your firm is short on experience in an area, a client that knows and trusts you is the one most likely to give you a chance in it. Parsons Brinckerhoff, for example, bid on a project to do permitting, right-of-way acquisition and design of a major fiber optic network. The firm's proposal stated forthrightly that it had no telecommunications industry experience and explained why that wasn't important. When PB's chairman, Bob Prieto, called the client to ask for his reaction to the proposal, the client responded, "There is only one weakness—you have no telecom experience." Ultimately, however, the firm won because the client had worked with PB for many years and knew it would work hard to make the project succeed.

The ability to stay with a client until it is ready to hire you for other work. If a client is likely to have an occasional need for your service, or changes service providers from time to time, introducing other services your firm offers can help you develop relationships and maintain contacts with your clients until they need what you offer. Joe Buskuhl of HKS Architects, Inc. notes that interior design services often provide this value to architects. "If there is a downturn and a client doesn't need a new building for a while, interiors continue to do well because clients tend to change their needs within their buildings. The key is to find a way to stay in touch with the client to maintain relationships with the right people, and learn about new projects as they come along." Similarly, an accounting firm that wants a client's audit work would be wise to sell it tax assistance, some other services, first as a way to get in the door and build relationships.

Selling more services to existing accounts can produce huge benefits to you and to your clients. It's little wonder that there is so much interest in the subject at professional firms.

Cross selling is also important to professionals on a personal level, as well. The ability to sell the full range of your firm's services is a route to promotion at most companies. Those serving in the most senior positions tend to be skilled at cross selling. Many firms reward their professionals with bonuses and promotions for bringing colleagues from other practices into their accounts. As one consultant told me, "Our own practice was so short of resources, the only way I could keep selling was to bring in other services." He has done well both financially and in terms of promotions.

This book is all about cross selling and how to reap the benefits of selling more work to your existing clients. Professionals typically think of three kinds of cross selling:

1. Selling multiple services to a single client.
2. Selling services to different business units of the same account.
3. Selling services to the same account in different regions.

For most firms, the single major reason to offer multiple services or have multiple offices is to provide these capabilities. Otherwise, why not just offer a single service from one office and do a superior job of providing it? Housing several services in one firm or having several offices implies that both the clients and owners will benefit. The ability to cross sell is so important, it can dwarf other benefits, such as greater purchasing power and stronger brand image.

Because it is a related subject, this book will also address in-selling, or selling extension services to those a client is currently buying. Much of what applies to cross selling applies to in-selling, too.

Aimed at professionals—accountants, actuaries, architects, attorneys, consulting engineers, executive recruiters, industrial designers, interior designers, lawyers, management consultants, public relations specialists, and the like—this book will benefit those who recognize that cross selling and in-selling are vital to provide greater value to clients, to advance their careers, and to improve their firms' financial performance.

It will also provide valuable ideas for those who manage other kinds of organizations, where a variety of technically strong people who work closely with customers can identify opportunities to sell more products and services. Hardware and software manufacturers with large service organizations are excellent examples of such organizations. Some of the examples in this book are drawn from such firms.

Most of the above already know that cross selling and in-selling can work because they have seen its results. But they may be having difficulty overcoming obstacles to achieving more success. These obstacles operate at three levels: the levels of the individual, the firm, and the client.

Functional Thinking

The most visible and discussed obstacles are those of the individual professional. Many of these obstacles derive from one source, which I will call "functional thinking." Most successful professionals spend a large part of their careers as specialists. Securities lawyers, tax accountants, executive compensation consultants, bridge designers, and many hundreds of other kinds of specialists devote years to learning about their fields and are rightly proud of their knowledge. Without the time and effort they have dedicated to their specialties, they couldn't provide the value to their clients and their firms that they do.

But specialization comes at a cost—the lack of breadth that limits their ability to cross sell. This may happen in several ways. First, specialists spend much of their time talking with people who are interested in the same kind of problem they specialize in, to the exclusion of others. This often means that they don't know many of the people at their client companies who buy other kinds of services. Even if they do, they don't feel comfortable talking to them about other kinds of problems. As a partner at a consulting firm said:

> Our people operate in functional silos. Our logistics people, for example, talk with their clients' logistics people. They have difficulty talking with the Chief Information Officer (CIO) and even more difficulty talking with the Chief Executive Officer (CEO), unless they, too, want to talk about logistics. Specialists don't have the breadth of interests to hold the right kind of conversation or to earn trust outside of logistics. But it is the CEOs and other executives who can hire us for other services. Those who are good at cross selling have broken out of the functional silo, or never thought that way in the first place.

Spending little time with colleagues in other practices leads to a lack of good information about their firms' other services. In fact, isolationists wouldn't recognize an opportunity for another practice if they stepped on it!

While functional thinking is usually benign, it also has a pathogenic form. A professional may deliberately ignore all potential to bring in colleagues from other practice areas out of fear that doing so could backfire. One professional told me:

> The last time I brought another practice into [my largest account] they did a lousy job and it almost cost me the relationship. Their entire fee was $75,000, but I almost lost a relationship worth a million and a half a year. It will be a long time before I make that mistake again.

The speaker failed to note that the $75,000 project did not benefit him financially, while the $1.5 million relationship accounted for a large part of his bonus. Although we might disagree with his conclusion, we can easily grasp the logic of his argument.

In worse cases, a professional will promote his practice's functional service, even though the client really needs a broader array of the firm's services to fully solve a problem. Why? The smaller sale is easier to make and more certain than opening up a discussion of larger issues. Selling the functional solution may also be more profitable for the practice because it may require more of the practice's services than a cross-functional one. Or the professional may simply want to control the account. Technically strong, such people enjoy showing off their knowledge and promote only their particular services.

For example, a newly hired partner at a large professional firm was assigned to an account team. The client, a rapidly growing corporation, only bought one of the firm's many services, and the new partner was expected to introduce others. She quickly learned that the partner in charge of the account didn't want her help. He always had an excuse about why he couldn't introduce her to anyone at the client.

Researching the company, she found that she knew a senior person there and called him. It had been intended as a low-key conversation just to catch up, but after they had talked for a while, the man began to complain about the way her firm was providing its services.

> He said that we were making decisions that they should be involved in. They felt that the partner in charge of the work acted as if he were smarter than they were and always knew best. They wanted more teamwork. They wanted more services that they weren't comfortable talking to him about.
>
> I almost got killed because I was new to the firm and it looked like I was just trying to take an account away from someone else.

But the client was adamant about having the current account manager replaced, and so he was. Within a year the professional firm had increased its sales to the client five-fold and was selling an array of services there worth many millions of dollars. If a control freak manages an account, often no one else in the firm knows if the client is happy or not. The only one they ask is the account manager, and in a control freak's mind, all his clients are happy.

Functional thinking is not the only reason why individual professionals fail to cross sell services; many also lack fundamental sales skills. This book will provide guidance to individual professionals on how to overcome these and other obstacles to cross-selling success.

Institutional Obstacles

As easy as it is to blame individual professionals for the lack of cross selling, management has a major responsibility to make it happen. It has three tools at its disposal for doing so, and one or more of these are underutilized at most firms.

The first is strong sales and account management. Sales and account management are badly underdeveloped functions at most professional service firms when compared to the same functions at traditional product companies. For decades, selling was a taboo subject in the professions. True professionals, it was said, don't sell; work comes to them because of their reputations. Versions of this mindset still exist in some professions.[1]

This view is dying out; many firms, for example, provide their people with one or more kinds of sales training. However, the development of sales and account management is still in its infancy, its development retarded by the absence of sales as a separate organizational function in the professions.

Most firms still operate under the "seller-doer" model—the people who sell work are also expected to do the work. Management is organized by functional practice, by geography, or by industry. In this environment, sales and account management can only be set up as one more factor in an already complex matrix, or as an additional responsibility for people who also do other things.

Unfortunately, the latter is overwhelmingly the choice. Because nobody has the clear and dedicated responsibility to develop the function, it is starved for attention. Parts of this book are about how the appropriate use of sales and account management can overcome the obstacles individual professionals face in cross selling and in-selling.

Second, firm communications, both external with clients and internal with firm professionals, can also be set up to foster cross selling. If done at all, this is often done haphazardly. One common approach is to gather representatives of different practices in a room and have each give a presentation on his or her practice. Management hopes that the knowledge participants pick up this way will enable them to cross sell. But by the middle of the second presentation, everyone's mind is wandering. Mentally, they are off skiing in Colorado or with a client hashing out a problem.

Firm communications is not my specialty, so I have asked an expert in the subject to contribute a chapter on it.

Third, for cross selling to work, a reward system must encourage it. To a degree, people do what you pay them to do. If your reward system doesn't support cross selling and in-selling, you face a major obstacle. As an attorney at one large firm said:

> When you really look at our compensation and promotion systems, people are rewarded for billability. Associates are rewarded for their own billability, and partners for theirs and that of the people who report to them. Helping another practice land a client does nothing financially for a person, it just takes time away from billing.

It's little wonder that the attorneys at this firm don't cross sell. An expert on compensation at professional firms has also contributed to a chapter on how compensation can encourage cross selling.

Client Resistance

A major obstacle to cross selling lies with the client. David Maister has pointed out that whatever the benefits of cross selling to professionals, unless it benefits the client it is unlikely to happen.[2]

Most large corporations are sophisticated buyers of professional services and are aware that professionals want to stay once they are invited in. As one professional said:

> The biggest obstacle to cross selling is that clients are aware that you have this mandate. They feel that as soon as you sell them one job, you will try to sell them another one. I have had clients tell me, "Don't expect to move in here. I want the work done and then I want you out."
>
> If cross selling is your intention, you won't achieve it. The client's best interests must be your number one priority.

Pressure companies feel to buy fewer services from their auditors compounds this problem. Still, clients can benefit from cross selling in several ways:

A holistic solution. A client may need multiple services to solve a problem. In fact, some professional firms are built around such cases, with architectural/engineering firms being an obvious example. When a client needs a new building, both architectural and engineering services will be needed.

A greater assurance of good work. Clients expect that professionals will work hard to ensure that a project goes well. If something goes wrong, they will work even harder to make it right, rather than endanger a large relationship. They also have faith that the professional who sold "service A" will select the best possible talent from the firm's stable of professionals to provide "service B." One lawyer said, "The general counsel [of an energy company] said that she relies on me for referrals because she knows I will send her the best person every time."

Easier approval. Where there is a close relationship between a senior executive at "company X" and a professional at "firm Y," word sometimes goes out that if you want to hire a professional, it will be easier to get approval if you use "firm Y." One professional ran a series of workshops for the newly hired CEO of a company. She had known the CEO for years. "[The executives who attended the workshops] could sense my relationship with the CEO at these sessions. They could see us conferring at breaks and over lunch. They realized that it would be easier to get approval for the expenditure if they came to me. At the same time, the CEO knew that my primary focus was to help his staff."

Getting work done faster. By using a firm that is already familiar to an organization, a client can often move faster. Jack Jolls of the consulting engineering firm Weston & Sampson cited such a case: "The head of the public works department had a backlog of projects, but the board was unwilling to give him money until he could get the projects he was already working on under construction. He wanted to get things moving quickly, and by coming to us, he cut two months out of the process because he didn't have to go out to procurement again."

Such things do happen, but just as often the client views a professional firm as specialists only in the area for which it was originally hired. "We are seen primarily as a litigation firm," one lawyer noted. "Our litigation clients don't want to consider us for corporate work."

Also, the buyer of "service A" may resent it when the professional she hired wants to sell "service B" to someone else in the company. The buyer fears that she will no longer receive the full attention of her primary contact. When there are hostilities between a client's department heads, a professional seen as allied with one department may be *persona non grata* with the other. For years a firm that consulted to one half of a large consumer goods company was blocked from selling services to the other half for this reason. There are many such examples.

This book will show how to identify situations where the client will benefit from cross selling and show how to make the client aware of these benefits.

In short, this book is a manual on cross selling. It will show how you can realize the benefits of cross selling and how to overcome the obstacles in many cases. You can use this guide in two ways: First, read it all the way through to fully understand how cross selling works, and how to do it. Later, you can refer back to it as a source of ideas when you wish to try cross selling.

The book is divided into two parts. Part I describes secrets of those who are successful at cross selling. Part II explores what your firm should do to make cross selling work, and what individual professionals should do to prepare themselves for cross-selling success.

I hope the methods described here will be used by professionals who always put their clients' interests first. I have included a final chapter on the ethics of cross selling to make these issues clearer for readers who are appropriately concerned about them.

Part I

The BEST Selling Model for Cross-Selling Success

To become more successful at cross selling, let's examine exactly what professionals who are good at cross selling do. Our research shows that they all use approaches that have many things in common. These elements can be captured in a model, which I call BEST Selling. This part of the book explains the model and offers evidence and examples to support it.

Once we understand how professionals cross sell successfully, we can look at what we need to do to apply the model as individuals, or to institute it within our firms. That will be the subject of Part II.

1

What Is Cross Selling?

Professionals, like others who sell, love to tell stories about their big sales. These stories deal with a subject vital to their success—the acquisition of clients—and are full of risks and unexpected events that make good fodder for storytelling. Professionals also like listening to such stories, in part because they reveal a lot about how to handle challenging sales situations.

In his book, *Sources of Power: How People Make Decisions*, Gary Klein[1] shows how policemen, firefighters, and others who must make life-or-death decisions in split seconds use stories to educate each other. The same approach can help to show how a large sale is made at a professional firm. A story about how a professional made contact with the key decision-maker at a critical moment, or how she earned the support of a client who had previously been a skeptic, grabs attention. Such stories also educate. Take these true stories, for example (names changed):

Cross selling has a lot to do with how you manage an existing client relationship. We designed a storm-water pipeline for the

Town of Sinnipset. During construction we learned that the contractor had ordered insufficient pipe to complete the job because of an error in our work. This resulted in an unexpected cost for the client of $50,000 for the extra pipe. The client suffered no financial damage—the pipe would have been required in any event—so they couldn't sue us, but no one likes this kid of surprise. When we discovered the problem we went to the head of the public works department and explained what had happened. We also sent a letter saying we had made an error, even though our lawyers told us not to, and offered some free design work to make up for it. When another big project came along, the head of the public works department was willing to hire us again. (*Partner at a civil engineering firm*)

A hip-hop artist in his twenties, who both performs and produces, made over $50 million last year. He hired us to work on some tax problems. We sat down with him for a simple discussion so that we would understand his business. During that meeting we learned that many of his tax problems resulted from his having inadequate financial controls and incomplete information. This resulted in his assigning us more work to help set up those controls, so he wouldn't have problems in the future. (*An accountant*)

A banker client of mine was offered a new position working on project financing in Latin America. I wanted to stay in touch with him, even though there probably wouldn't be any work for me in his new area, so I invited him to lunch, just to catch up, and took a lawyer with experience in project finance in Latin America with me. It was a low-key way to introduce her without putting pressure on the client. In a few days I got a call back from another woman at the bank with a project finance issue, though it wasn't in Latin America. I know where that call came from. I believe that eventually we will do work on Latin American projects, too. (*A bankruptcy attorney*)

In addition to being interesting, these stories provide clear messages about client relationships and cross selling:

1. Be forthright with clients about mistakes, and it will be easier to get additional work.
2. Understand the client's business, rather than just focus on the technical problem you were hired to solve.
3. Once you have a good relationship with a client, don't let it fade, even if, in his new job, it seems unlikely that he will need your specific services again.

As valuable as these messages might be, they don't reveal what is involved in turning a small project into a large account. Nor do they say much about how to move from providing one service to providing several services for a client.

Ask a professional to describe how he did one of these things and you run into a problem: Much of the good stuff gets left out. The professional will say that the firm "started with a small analysis that I sold to an old friend who had called me with a question. That led to a second project where we . . ." The phrase *that led to* abbreviates the actions we are interested in. By asking the professional to elaborate on these abbreviations, you can extract a more complete story, like this one told to me by a health care consultant (names have been changed):

We were hired to conduct a facilities planning study for Bamburgh, one hospital in a large university hospital system. We knew there could be a lot of work at this organization for all of our practices, and we knew specifically that another hospital in the system, Bristol, would need to be replaced soon.

Knowing from the start that there was a big opportunity for us to do more work, we devoted a portion of our regular project meetings to identifying additional opportunities to help the client and to figuring out how to go after them. We realized that there were four or five key people at the client's office that we needed to get to, and set up a communications plan to make that happen.

Because it would make the project run more smoothly and because it would also further our goals to get to know key people at the hospitals, we set up a weekly steering committee meeting which we asked these people to attend. Among other questions, we asked the new committee members about the best place to locate specific services. Should a specific service be located at Bamburgh or should it be located at Bristol, a community hospital? These were legitimate questions that needed answers, but also engaged us in discussions about Bristol and revealed the steering committee's need to know more about that facility.

During one of these meetings, we learned that the CEO and the head of the School of Medicine, two key players, met weekly. We arranged to meet with them once a month to report on our project and solicit their help. At these meetings, we would bring up things that we couldn't bring up at the steering committee meetings. We could raise issues that helped them realize that they needed to address additional concerns, such as the planning for a new facility at Bristol.

It became clear through this process that the planning involving the appropriate relationship between Bamburgh Hospital and others in the system, like Bristol, had been inadequate. We pointed out that decisions were being made that would affect the other hospitals, and that the administrators at these facilities would resent changes that would be perceived as being crammed down their throats, unless they were allowed to participate in the decisions. The CEO agreed that it was important to involve more people.

As a result, we set up fifteen task forces to deal with specific subjects, like education and clinical issues, and we staffed all of them. As a part of their jobs, the consultants who staffed the task forces were responsible for getting close to key members by having periodic value-added meetings. These task forces raised a number of issues that we could help address. For example, the education task force said it wanted to distribute more of the education process to train medical students throughout the system, instead of concentrating so much of it at Bamburgh. This choice had information technology implications, so we got our IT people involved.

As a part of this process, we got the chief administrator for Bristol on the steering committee. She was really happy with this because in the past Bamburgh had been the "800-pound gorilla," imposing its decisions on others without informing the people at Bristol in advance. One of our people met with her weekly to make sure she was up to speed on all the issues the task forces were dealing with. She liked this because it kept her better informed than she had ever been. When the time came to develop new plans for her hospital, she wanted to work with us.

As it became clear how the organization wanted to integrate the work of the different hospitals in the system, information technology issues became more and more important, and so the information technology task force's role became increasingly important. One of our IT people was staffing that task force, so when it came time to find resources that the CIO didn't have, they didn't even go out to bid. We got the work. Initially, this was work to integrate the Bamburgh and Bristol systems. But that led to us doing the client's Y2K work.

We have done a lot of work for this client and continue to talk about doing more.

This story gives a much clearer idea of how a group of professionals converted a relatively small, single-service project into a large multiservice account. There are multiple messages, some of which we will come back to later in this book:

- Cross selling is based on bringing value to the client team in ways they may not have expected when they hired you.
- Cross selling requires frequent contact with the key decision-makers at the client organization, and the key decision-makers for one service may differ from those that are key for another.
- Cross selling often requires helping the clients understand how decisions they are making in one area affect other issues and other parts of their organizations.

Also, the nature of the cross-selling process becomes clearer. It is fluid, requiring both planning and the ability to quickly adapt to events as they unroll. When a takeoff point appears to greatly increase the number and intensity of contacts between client and professional teams, this must be recognized and seized upon. In the story, this occurred when the fifteen task forces were formed.

Still, there are many places in this story where we would like more information. The consultant notes, for example, that he arranged to meet monthly with the CEO and the head of the School of Medicine. Exactly how did he arrange that? We could go on peeling back layer upon layer of such a story and keep learning interesting insights into the cross-selling process.

And that is what we did—for dozens and dozens of stories. From these stories we learned what cross selling is and how it works. We then analyzed successful cross-selling efforts and reduced what we learned to the model that is the subject of this book. This model, which we call BEST Selling, meets several important criteria. It is:

Simple. You must manage many complexities in the professional/client relationship over many months during the execution of a complicated project. Any cross-selling model must be easy to understand, remember, and apply, or professionals won't be able to use it.

Flexible. The marketplace presents you with a bewildering array of situations. Some industries are made up of many small players, while others have but two or three major ones. Some companies are highly centralized, while others are decentralized. Sometimes you'll come in at the top of the client organization; at other times, you may not. Some clients are open to using professionals for a broad array of work, while some others want to use them for specific tasks. The list of ways that clients and their situations can differ from each other is infinite. Any cross-selling model must be flexible enough to be adaptable to almost any situation the market requires.

Practical and action-oriented. Many account management programs are planning-oriented. They assume that action will follow because these programs are designed for organizations that have dedicated sales forces whose primary job is to sell. But most professionals are seller/doers who must execute client work as well as sell it. Though account planning is important, the model must help ensure that action follows. This prevents the pressure to turn out work from driving out the time needed to cross sell.

We believe the BEST Selling Model meets these criteria because it reflects what professionals who are good at cross selling actually do. The criteria are imposed by the circumstances that professionals must deal with and so shape the way they behave.

We also studied many cross-selling failures. In most of these cases, it was clear that the professionals involved hadn't used the BEST Selling Model. They had failed, if you will forgive the pun, to follow BEST practices. In other cases, they had tried to follow the required practices but had failed.

Before describing the model, we must make clear what "cross selling" means. Our research shows that the term is used to describe three related but different things.

The first is *selling to an unrelated need*. This occurs when a professional working with a client in one area, such as a lawyer working on an intellectual capital issue, hears of an entirely unrelated need that the client has that his firm might be able to help with, such as a labor law issue. Inexperienced professionals sometimes think that this is what cross selling is primarily about. It isn't. While such sales are made, they are the most difficult kind of cross sale. The client has no reason to believe that your expertise in the area where you are currently working translates into expertise in the new area. Your pursuit of the second opportunity may seem opportunistic, which, in fact, it is, though in the better sense of the word.

Also, the buyers of the two services are likely to be different people. Your current contact at the client may not be able or willing to help you pursue the second opportunity. This explains why an engineer, Emad Youssef of PS&S, pursued a large pharmaceuticals company the way he did:

We had a series of geotechnical projects for this client, but only geotechnical work, and our people provided excellent service on them. I wanted to expand the relationship so that we could help this client with architectural and mechanical, electrical, civil, and structural engineering needs, too. To do this, I started asking around to see who ran multi-disciplined projects at the client's company. When I had identified these project managers,

I made cold calls to them. It took a lot of calls to get meetings. Once we were in the door, my partners and I would tell these project managers about the geotechnical work we were performing for their company. They called their colleagues for references on us and heard good things. I had never asked their colleagues for referrals because they saw us purely as geotechnical experts.

One presentation was to the head of engineering services. After that presentation, we started to get work in other areas. The buyers of these services told us that they knew we were doing good and profitable geotechnical work, but that if we messed up in the other areas, we would lose the whole account. We worked hard building these relationships, and now we provide the full range of our services. The company is now one of our major clients.

Cold calling is not typically associated with cross selling. Youssef took this approach because he was selling to unrelated needs, but there are other approaches.

A second kind of cross selling is *Selling Upstream or Downstream*. In these cases, a professional uncovers needs that must be addressed downstream or upstream of his current work. For example, a consultant helping to design a new warehouse may learn that the client's current inventory management system won't work with the new design. Alternatively, the consultant may help the company realize that before the warehouse can be designed, the client needs to decide which products to ship from which warehouses, (i.e., that a logistical analysis is required).

This is probably the most common kind of cross selling. It only requires the professional to know about those services most clearly linked to her own, and allows her to continue with her own project pretty much without complication. The result is typically sequential selling: "project A" leads to "project B" and "project B" leads to "project D."

Though this can be effective, there are situations in which it shouldn't be applied. The client may feel badly used if the professional's work never seems to end. Each time the client gets close to finishing a project, he learns that another phase is required to capture full value. Worse, the client may reject a phase and so fail to capture full value from those that have been completed.

Still, selling upstream and downstream can be highly beneficial to the client and to the professional. Forensic accountant Wayne Hoeberlein of Kroll provided a good example:

> A diversified holding company bought another outfit and, after the purchase closed, suspected they were paying an inflated price and that something was wrong with the books. We were brought in to analyze the books. It was a pure forensic case. The former owners were entitled to a higher payout if they achieved a performance trigger point. After they made their numbers in accordance with this agreement, there were a lot of write-offs. There were also sales on the books that had never been made. If accounted for properly, these two items would have pushed the income below the trigger point.

> On the basis of this work, we were able to sell background checks on the former owners. The client realized that he needed to know more about these guys and asked us what we could do. I said we could do a lot. The background checks provided a good picture of the kind of people he was dealing with.

The third kind of cross selling is *selling an integrated solution*. The professional helps the client see that solving a problem will require a cross-functional approach, usually through multiple subprojects and phases. For example, the client may talk with a technology consultant about establishing an online ordering system for its customers. During the meeting, the consultant may show the client that, for maximum advantage, a full supply-chain strategy and implementation will be required. This will lead to several new projects. The projects may roll out one at a time, in a manner similar to the way those sold downstream do, but all of the projects are sold, at least in concept and in the broad outline of their pricing, at the beginning of the engagement. Ian B. Wilson of PricewaterhouseCoopers describes this approach:

> Increasingly clients have problems that no one service can solve. Formerly, we were organized by service line and sold that way. We would ask if a client wanted some process redesign. Often, they didn't. Today, we go to market on an issue so we get pulled in by the client. We put together the services first and may then offer two or three different approaches to solve a problem. Our objective is to sell the full answer on Day One, so the client doesn't feel he is being cross sold, but rather that he is dealing with people who are committed to meeting his needs.

The value of an integrated solution for the client is clear in this story told by Bruce Beverly of the geotechnical engineering and environmental consulting firm Haley & Aldrich:

> [A well-known eastern college] was under pressure to do an environmental cleanup of undeveloped portions of the campus. Environmental investigations by other firms had been costly and had extended over several years. College officials were frustrated that all this work still hadn't provided cleanup solutions.
>
> Members of our staff knew the college's attorney and contractor, and we were given an opportunity to present a solution-based approach instead of just another investigation.
>
> Two professionals from our firm, one a specialist in underground engineering and the other an environmental professional, worked together to learn what had already been done by the other firms. This team showed the client that we could both

design and implement a solution that integrated an environmental cleanup with the desired expansion of the campus.

People want solutions for their problems, not just studies from individual disciplines. The problem required a multidisciplinary approach, and to solve it we offered a team that had worked together before on similar issues and had a proven track record of success.

This is the most sophisticated kind of cross sale and requires the deepest understanding of the client's business issues. The benefit to the client is usually great. But selling an integrated solution may be difficult or even impossible, if your contact at the client is a functional specialist. He may not have either the interest or the influence to help you sell at the high level an integrated solution requires.

A skilled cross seller can often get around this problem. One firm we know almost always enters a client company at middle- and lower-management levels. Their initial contacts are functional specialists. Often, they end up working at top management levels on an integrated solution worth millions of dollars in fees.

An approach to cross selling must be able to handle these three kinds of opportunity. The remainder of this book will tell what we learned from our research about how successful professionals cross sell.

2

How Rainmakers Do It: An Overview of the BEST Selling Model

B EST is an acronym, which stands for buyers, events, signals, and techniques. While executing the initial project, the professional cross sells by managing these four elements, as shown in the four boxes at the center of Exhibit 2.1

This chapter provides an overview of the BEST Selling Model. You'll find details on individual components in succeeding chapters.

In most cases, cross selling begins after a firm is already working for a client. The first assignment can be for almost any service a firm offers. At most firms, however, there are a small number of services that their clients are most likely to buy initially, or which are most likely to convert to larger, multiservice relationships. Recognizing this, some firms have been particularly astute at developing services to obtain this initial entry. I will call a service that is deliberately used to gain entry a "portal project."[1] Such a service must provide stand-alone value to the client. It must also give the professional opportunities to meet a variety of potential buyers within the client company. Portal projects are often, though not always, some form of diagnostic. They are the subject of Chapter 3.

Exhibit 2.1
BEST Selling Model

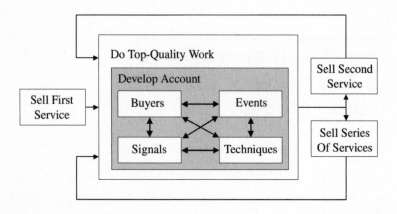

Source: Harding & Company

As a foundation for cross selling, the professional must do excellent work during the initial project. This point came up again and again in the interviews with the rainmakers who cross sold into major accounts:

First, you have to solve the specific issue you were brought in to solve. You have to jump over the bar with room to spare. But you also have to be alert for other opportunities. (*A consultant*)

We did good work [on an initial project], and they were very pleased with it. We treated them well. They told me, "We want to be treated like one of our accountant's best clients. We aren't sure we're treated that way [by our current auditors] even though we're a billion-and-a-half-dollar company." We made sure they realized that we thought of them as one of our most important clients. (*An accountant*)

We really, really tried to show them how committed we were to their success. We used the "pint-of-blood" metaphor to describe it. The operations guy we were working for said he could rely on us to get things done. That's the base we built from. (*A consultant*)

[The state university] had built a succession of science buildings that hadn't turned out well. They wouldn't work right for the scientists without a lot of startup problems. Ours did work. Our team delivered a quality building from top to bottom. If you have done well for your first client, they become your references for your second, third, fourth, and fifth project. The success of this building enabled us to go on and do five other buildings for this university, even though we were from out of state and the governor had said he wanted all work to be done by architectural firms based in the state. (*An architect*)

I started working with [a discount clothing retailer] as an associate and tried a burn case for them, which had a good outcome. The work built from there. (*A lawyer*)

We worked hard to make sure that the [first] project was a success. The results were amazing for them. (*A consultant*)

We got some good coverage for the head of the financial institutions practice quite quickly. He walked into an executive committee meeting and threw down the clippings and said, "I don't know if you have had anything like this. I haven't before, and it's making my life much easier." So after that we began to work in other parts of the organization. (*A public relations specialist*)

We were providing structural work as a subcontractor to an architect on a project for a large developer. The construction manager was unhappy with the work the civil engineering firm was doing and, because of the good structural work we had done, asked if we did civil engineering, too. This eventually turned into a big civil and environmental site-engineering project. (*An engineer*)

If you don't do excellent work during your first assignment, the client will have little interest in working with you in other areas. We will not dwell on this issue further because we assume that you know how to deliver top-quality service.

The professionals working an initial project make a point of meeting potential buyers of the services they offer. All good sales planning programs help sellers identify different kinds of buyers. In their classic work, *Strategic Selling,* for example, Robert Miller and Stephen Heiman talk about four kinds of buyers: economic buyers, user buyers, technical buyers, and coaches.[2] I highly recommend this book for anyone interested in becoming a skilled seller.

Because we are dealing specifically with cross selling, we categorize buyers somewhat differently, as cross-functional buyers, functional buyers, bridge buyers, and information sources. These buyers will be discussed in more detail in Chapter 4. For now, it is enough to say that professionals who are good cross sellers deliberately find ways to meet all kinds of buyers during the initial assignment.

Alert sellers meet buyers at *events* (see Chapter 5), usually a meeting with a buyer or buyers, though it can occasionally be a phone call. Broadly speaking, there are two kinds of events: those that take place as a part of paid work for a client, and those that don't. The kinds of events required to complete an assignment vary from profession to profession and from firm to firm and practice to practice. In all cases, they include fact-finding meetings and review meetings. Unlike other professionals, cross sellers use events to meet and to develop relationships with buyers that they might otherwise have difficulty getting to know. When they can't meet someone they need to know in the context of paid work, they find another way to meet him or her. So, for example, many firms run seminars on subjects of interest to their clients in hopes that people they want to meet will attend.

At these events, professionals look for *signals* (see Chapter 6). Signals are indications that clients need additional services. There are two kinds of signals, *macro-signals* and *micro-signals*. Macro-signals are major changes at a client organization that will drive the need for many services. They include mergers, acquisitions, the appointment of a new CEO, and a major change in stock price.

Micro-signals are signals specific to a particular practice. The signals that indicate the need for an information technology project differ from those calling for a need for a regulatory impact assessment. Those that indicate the potential for a labor law case will differ from those requiring an environmental law case. The micro-signals for a structural engineering project differ from those for an electrical engineering project. Although usually found in what people say, signals can also be found in visible clues. Rainmakers listen and look for signals at every event with every buyer. More than that, they deliberately work to help signals surface.

Signals are surfaced by using *techniques* (see Chapter 7). Techniques are tactics that a professional uses to raise a signal, obtain an event, or obtain a commitment for additional work. For example, Joe Caso, while working for a large accounting firm, would often start a relationship with a client by selling a small project, usually a tax accounting project. In the course of this work, it was easy to get the client to talk about the current auditor. As a casual aside, Caso would then say, "I'm sure you're happy with your auditor." Sometimes the client would respond, "Don't be so sure of that." Caso used this simple technique to surface a signal that the client might like to find a new auditor.

As the chart shows, the four elements of the BEST Selling Model are closely interrelated. You first obtain events from buyers, and you meet buyers at events. You then obtain signals from buyers at events and these signals indicate which events, with which buyers, you might want to arrange in the future. You use techniques with buyers at events to obtain signals and to obtain future events. The buyers you are working with and signals you obtain from them suggest what techniques to use to advance the sale. If you have enough events with enough buyers, and obtain enough signals and use the right techniques, additional work is likely to follow. Once you obtain a second assignment or series of assignments, the process begins all over again. That is how cross selling is done.

The approach is simple, flexible, and practical—and it can be managed. But that doesn't make it easy to do in the dynamic and complex context of working with a large client. Each month you can review which buyers you met over the past thirty days, at which events, and what signals you have obtained. Then, you can plan for the next month, asking yourself which buyers you need to get to, what events you can schedule with them, and which techniques you will use at those events to elicit signals or to advance the sale.

Here is another cross-selling story, a relatively simple one, annotated to highlight the elements of the BEST Selling Model. It was told to me by Barry Seymour, now with the large engineering firm Black & Veatch, but at the time he was with a regional firm in Michigan that was seeking to expand into industrial markets.

We had tried to get into [a large plant of a major automobile supplier] for over two years. We had made presentation after presentation and submitted proposal after proposal, but always came in fourth or fifth. Finally, we started asking what kinds of problems they were having (*at an event, presumably a sales call*). The plant engineer (*buyer*) told us they were having problems with lab analyses of their wastewater discharge. Whenever they sent samples to Indiana for analysis, the results kept coming back late. We told them of our lab capabilities, and soon they visited our lab *(event)*. We pointed out that because we were so close to them, they wouldn't have to ship samples to us; we could easily pick them up.

After that visit they gave us our first job *(portal project)*, a small analysis worth about $2,500. We gave them really good service, and from then on the lab analysis work grew until we were getting most of it.

The plant engineer was authorized to buy services for up to $15,000. If a project cost more than that, he needed the approval of the plant manager *(buyer)*. We knew we would have to get to him, but first we worked hard to develop the relationship with the plant engineer because we needed his support to get more work. He said he really appreciated the service he was getting.

I would stop by and meet with him *(events)*, and sometimes we would go to the cafeteria for lunch *(event)*. I would ask him what was going on *(questioning technique)*. One day he mentioned that they were "being killed" by the EPA and the local municipal wastewater treatment authority *(signal)*. The city's rates for treating wastewater at the municipal treatment facility included a surcharge if the strength of the company's wastewater exceeded an agreed-upon level, which it often did.

I mentioned that we had helped an industrial client with a similar problem in Detroit *(technique)*. He asked to hear more about what we had done. I said I could bring in the people who had done that work who could tell him more about it *(technique)* and he agreed. We had the meeting *(event)*, and he liked what he heard. Then, we assessed how we could treat his wastewater to avoid surcharges, how much the company would save, and what the payback would be on the investment required to fix the problem *(technique)*. After that he asked for a proposal.

Of course, he couldn't authorize a project of this size by himself, so he helped us get a meeting *(event)* with the plant manager. Several other people had to buy into the project, too, and the plant engineer helped us get meetings with them as well *(event)*. After that, we were delighted to be hired on a sole source basis *(second service)*.

We proceeded to design an air flotation treatment system, which our client was really pleased with. The oil their new system recovered from their wastewater was of such high quality they could use it for fuel to heat the building. The payback was even faster than we had estimated.

We continued meeting *(events)* with their people *(buyers)* during this project, getting to know them really well. At one of the meetings, they revealed that they were putting in a new over-head crane *(signal)* and needed help with the structural work. It was a small retrofit, but it demonstrated yet another one of our services *(third service)*.

This example makes the BEST Selling process look simple. In fact, the process is fairly straightforward. The challenge is in the execution. The following chapters show how each element of the BEST Selling Model creates building blocks for its successful execution.

3

Portal Projects: Getting in the Door

When one financial services company acquired another, the chairman of PricewaterhouseCoopers offered the services of Rocco Maggiotto, then managing partner of the Financial Services Consulting Practice, to help integrate the two organizations. Maggiotto's time was donated at no charge. For the next few months, Maggiotto devoted 50 percent of his time to this account, working with the client's top management team, fitting this work in with his other responsibilities. Every night, he met with the management team from 6:00 P.M. to 9:00 P.M. to sort out problems and plan the next day's effort. Often he left these meetings with assignments that had to be completed by 7:00 A.M. the next morning.

As Maggiotto says, "When you're building trust, you have to do whatever it takes. You have to demonstrate that you are a partner with them." Maggiotto worked with the client management on day-to-day integration issues while developing an overall response to the longer-term challenges of the acquisition.

The client understood that though Maggiotto's services were free, PricewaterhouseCoopers would charge if they brought in other people. In a merger there is plenty to do, so the client eventually did need additional people with specific skills. Maggiotto was now well positioned to provide what was needed. PricewaterhouseCoopers brought in consultants, tax specialists, and business assurance specialists with industry expertise on complex issues, along with junior auditors to do arms-and-legs accounting and control tasks. This freed up the client's staff to do more critical work.

Sometimes during one of the evening meetings, it became clear that the client would need immediate help from PricewaterhouseCoopers' financial services specialists. Maggiotto was the "can-do" man, delivering the extra help, often by early the next morning. He now had the authority to get his contacts to commit their best talent quickly. The higher the quality of work these people provided, the more his client trusted him. Equally important, using PricewaterhouseCoopers saved the company time because it didn't have to vet alternative providers.

The merger was a success for the client, and by its completion PricewaterhouseCoopers had earned large fees across the firm for tax, audit, and consulting work. "When you have a good relationship, there is little question about paying, as long as the clients feel they're getting value for their money," concludes Maggiotto.

Offering Maggiotto's time for free was a tactical move that paid off handsomely for both the client and PricewaterhouseCoopers. This is an example of a "portal project," a small, low-cost service that brings a professional inside the client's organization. From this vantage point, it is possible to cross sell other services. Portal projects go by many other names, including "wedges," "trial engagements," and "relationship starters." One professional we interviewed referred to them as "x-rays." Some firms use a specific type of portal project repeatedly, dubbing it a "diagnostic," a "benchmark," or a "walk through."

Sometimes these services are delivered free and sometimes for a fee. All portal projects, however, provide value to the client—well in excess of their cost. The value to the professional is clear. Professionals we interviewed consistently used similar words to describe that value:

- [The portal project] gets you inside—walking the halls, talking to people—instead of standing on the outside trying to figure out how to get in. (*An accountant*)
- Get in whatever door you can [e.g., sell whatever service you can] and then wander around inside. (*A lawyer*)
- It's about purposeful wandering around. You're in there in delivery mode [on a first assignment], and that delivery leads you to talk to people who are peripheral to the main business you are working on. They can be in a supply unit or a staff department. When you talk to them about the issue you have been hired for, you learn how they do business in broad terms. You learn about their issues. You say a few things that are provocative and come back later and talk with them, and a relationship gets built and eventually another opportunity arises. (*A management consultant*)

By talking with people at the client's location, you learn a lot about the client's situation. Yes, you can get information through external research, and you should. But the information you get from talking with people is qualitatively different. As Dwight Davies of Deloitte Consulting says:

Unless you are talking with people at the client, you don't understand who's under pressure and who's not. You won't understand organizational politics or budgets and the availability of funds or the position of your competitors or who is aligned with whom.

At any given time, there is a set of challenges that a company has agreed to work on. Say they've targeted five things. They're not always the obvious five things. If you are talking to people about one of those five things, you are helping them. If you're not talking about one of those five things, you're an outsider. Talking with people is the best way to identify and understand the implications of those five things.

Here's an example: Big problems get broken into pieces and given to people. If the company is under a lot of pressure to cut costs, one person, say the head of customer care, may be asked to reduce his budget by $300 million. *That's the specific piece of information you need to know.* The more you know about his stake, his relationships with competitors and with the people working with him, the better shot you have at getting the project that will help him.

The use of portals is simply one example of the well-documented practice of growing a relationship through incremental commitment.[1] Not all cross-selling efforts begin with a project specifically designated as a portal. In fact, any project that gets you inside talking with people will do—but many firms devote a lot of effort to designing portals. Here are some of their characteristics. Few portal projects meet all these criteria, but all meet a number of them.

They Are Clearly in the Client's Best Interest

As is the case with all professional work, if it's not in the client's best interest, you shouldn't do it. There is nothing deceptive about selling a portal project; it is unwise as well as unethical to begin your new relationship with a deception. Most professionals clearly state the introductory nature, using words such as, "This will allow you to see how we work and get to know us."

The project must provide real value to the client. As Tom Murnane, also with PricewaterhouseCoopers, says, "If your sole purpose is to get into a client to cross sell, you will fail. Clients are too smart for that and will cut you off at the knees. The primary goal has to be to do something in the best interests of the client. If you don't, they see it pretty fast."

The law firm Skadden Arps Meagher Slate & Flom used a portal service this way to grow from a specialty firm known for its mergers and acquisitions work to a much larger, broadly based firm. Skadden charged clients an annual retainer to reserve its services in case they became takeover targets, and it then allowed them to use this money to pay for any other legal services of the firm they might use. If, for example, the client used the firm for help with an environmental matter, the fee for the work could be taken from the retainer.

The firm got fair compensation from clients while demonstrating concern that its clients got value from the money they spent, even if they didn't become acquisition targets.[2]

They Don't Create Price Resistance

The fee on a portal project should not be so high that it creates price resistance. The goal is to get inside the client's organization, where you can show what value you can provide while learning about the client. The idea is not to make a large profit.

In some cases, this means that the service is offered free. Many lawyers, for example, offer a first consultation with a prospective client at no charge. Many re-engineering consultants provide clients with a free assessment of the level of costs that they can help cut. These assessments build a case for the cost reductions based on interviews, observations, and analyses conducted over a few days. Accountants will sometimes offer to evaluate a client's tax documents for free in order to identify opportunities where the client may save.

In other cases, a professional may charge for a service but often at lower than the normal rate. This is particularly true if substantial time is required for the work. One performance-improvement consulting firm puts a small team in place at the client organization for six to eight weeks at cost.

Generally, the more lucrative the project likely to flow out of the portal project, the more time and effort the professional will have to put into the portal. This time and effort is frequently offered to the client for free, or at a reduced rate as an inducement, an indication of the potential value of the budding association.

The client may also see the reduced fee as compensation for the learning curve required as the professional learns about the client's organization. As one client told a professional, "We have several of your competitors in here working with us already, and they have made a big investment in getting to know us. You can't expect to walk in here and get work without making an investment yourself."

Not all portal projects are discounted, however. A company can get full fee for a service, if it is a service that the firm is highly reputed for providing, and if the client wants that service now. We will come back to this point shortly.

They Allow You to Talk with the Right People in the Client Organization

Regardless of how it is priced, a portal project must give the professional an opportunity to talk with people in the client organization who may lead to more work for the professional. Most portal projects require extensive interviewing in the client organization. These interviews help the professional understand the issues facing individuals on the client team, and build commitment among the team members for further action.

The professional usually states why it is important to talk to key people. For example, when the head of distribution at a large retailer asked a consultant to help plan a new distribution center, the consultant suggested a short needs analysis as a first step. To design the new center, he and the head of distribution required a better understanding of the strategy behind the new business. That would require their meeting with the head of the new division and other key players, including the head of marketing and the head of merchandising.

It became clear in the interviews that no one had developed a clear strategy for the new business, so the consultant pointed out that it might be premature to design the distribution center in this vacuum. The company risked spending a lot of money on a facility that later might not meet its needs. The consultants were then hired to help develop a strategy for the whole division. By using the needs assessment to meet the key players in the client organization, the consultant was able to identify the client's real issue, then cross sold a major service that provided far more value than the distribution center project would have.

They Answer the Question(s) the Client Needs Answered Now

It is possible that a client may have a problem that will cost $20 million to fix but may not be willing to spend that money now. Even so, the client will have questions that need to be answered right now that can constitute a first step to solving the larger problem. Portal projects often answer those first few questions, immediately providing value to the client.

Most architectural firms offer facilities programming services. These give the client information on the amount and kinds of space a new building will contain. With this information, the client can develop budgets, schedules, and a request for a proposal. Site planning projects serve a similar function for a piece of land, providing essential information on infrastructure requirements, and building locations.

Alternatively, your contact in the client organization may not have the support or funds to take on a problem just now. Many portal projects help the client build commitment to the project, and ensure that funds are available. For example, few corporations had budgeted the dollars required to deal with the Year 2000 computer bug. Chief information officers were faced with the unenviable task of informing their bosses that they would have to spend millions of dollars to protect their systems or risk debilitating disruptions. The CEOs often found it hard to believe this news. Information technology consultants developed seminars, workshops, and diagnostics, all of which were designed to build awareness of the magnitude of the problem and a commitment to dealing with it, so that money would be found to finance the fix.

Much professional work is driven by specific events, such as a merger, an acquisition, a bankruptcy, a public offering, or a corporate relocation. Many firms that feed off such events develop portal projects to address the client's early concerns when first contemplating the event. A major software implementation is one example of a change that drives the need for technology consulting services. The consulting firm that helps the client select the best software package from an array of competing packages often has an edge on winning the implementation project.

Some professionals design services that allow them to work with the client *before* an issue arises. This can be particularly effective when the need for their services may be infrequent. Two litigators provide examples of such services:

We handle major litigation, but corporations don't have these kinds of cases every year. This means you may have long periods when you are not working for a client. To overcome this problem, I have volunteered to help clients deal with small, routine matters—such as a lawsuit being erroneously filed against a client, or something of that nature. In fact, I have helped set up a system for dealing efficiently with such repetitive cases. That really helps the client, and helps you stay in contact with and get closer to the people who retain litigators. (*David Keyko, Pillsbury Winthrop*)

We sometimes put one of our people in a client's shop two or three times a week to assess legal issues, so the issues don't get to a crisis point before being dealt with. That allows the client to access a lot of our resources. The day-to-day stuff like this is on a flat fee basis, which is more economical for them than calling a lawyer and asking questions. This arrangement also gives us insight into their issues and helps us develop a strong relationship. (*Beth Sher, Pitney Hardin Kipp & Szuch*)

They Provide Quick, Obvious Value to the Client

The value of some professional services is vague, such as a good employee medical plan or a well-designed building. In addition, the value of some services may take a long time to become apparent. A company may need a new strategy, but the value of that strategy will usually be seen over many years, not at the time the new strategy is developed. When the value to be received is nebulous or delayed, a client may be reluctant to hire an untested professional. In fact, it may decide not to hire at all.

Portal projects designed to provide fast, tangible value can solve both of these problems. The client can get to know the professional on a project where the value is clear and quickly received. The confidence the client develops in the professional will make it easier to approach the same person about a later offering with less clear, or more delayed, value.

The value provided by the portal project need not always be financial. Many years ago, Dan, a former client, came to me with an assignment that his boss, the chairman of his company, had handed him: Decide if the corporate headquarters should be relocated. Though we talked about the issues and our ability to help for some time, I sensed that Dan was not ready to hire us for the full project.

Then, clearly nervous, he admitted that he would have to sell the project to his company's board. The company was losing money, and the board might be skeptical about such an expensive undertaking. Yet the CEO had asked Dan to make a compelling case for exploring the issue. When I offered to help draft the presentation, Dan's relief was obvious. After he successfully made his case to the board, we were awarded the engagement.

They Don't Require Displacing the Current Service Provider

Most large organizations employ an accountant, an attorney, and an actuary. They are also using a variety of consultants and engineers on a number of projects. All of these professionals have established relationships with the client, and know the client's business and the specific problems they have been hired to address. They also know the personalities, aspirations, and fears of the people in the client organization whom they work with. Displacing them would incur a switching cost, which the client would be reluctant to pay.

Let us look at an example of a service provider whose replacement would create difficulties. Most companies are notoriously loyal to the actuaries who help administer their pension programs. In fact, the number of major companies that change actuaries in a year is probably less than a dozen. This is because of the complexity of most pension programs and the position of the buyers of pension advisory services within a corporate hierarchy.

Large organizations do not have a single, monolithic pension program; rather, they have an amalgam of systems built up over time through special programs. These are designed to meet past organizational needs, mergers, acquisitions, divestitures, and a range of other historical events. Often, the details of these special programs are poorly documented. A company might, for example, divest a business unit and still retain pension obligations to the people who worked there prior to the divestiture. Or, a company may create a contract with special pension features for an executive it wishes to hire. Once such deals are completed, the company may keep few detailed records on them, leaving that responsibility to its actuary.

Therefore, should the company decide to replace its current actuary, the newcomer will lack knowledge about the program, as well as its systems and data—information that allowed the previous actuary to work accurately and efficiently.

Let's say that Margo, an actuary, was hired to replace Walt, from another firm. She is given mounds of paper and electronic files to sort through and figure out how they all fit together. To clarify confusing and incomplete information, she is ultimately forced to contact two sources: the old actuary, who may not be overeager to help his replacement and may charge for his time to do so, or the administrator of the pension program at the client organization.

That person, too, is likely very busy or may be new to the job, and of little help. So working with a new actuary does not make life easier, unless the old firm was particularly uncooperative.

The person who administers a pension plan is not a corporate mover-and-shaker dealing with strategic issues. Rather, this person is a lower- to middle-level manager charged with looking after numerous administrative details shunned by higher-ups in the organization. His rewards come from delivering information promptly and accurately; he is largely invisible the rest of the time.

The nature of a pension administrator's responsibilities and rewards system tends to attract a person who is risk-averse. Yet this person has a lot of influence on which actuary gets hired. After all, he is one of the few people in a company with the technical knowledge to evaluate an actuary's competence, and his success in the organization is closely tied to how well the actuary does her job.

If the actuary is slow in providing information or provides inaccurate information, the consequences can be dire for the internal administrator. For example, if pension data needed to calculate quarterly returns is delayed or vague, this administrator is likely to get the first call. If the actuary inaccurately reports that the company has overfunded its pension, and then the company must make an unexpected payment later, it is, at best, embarrassing for the administrator.

If an executive considering retirement asks for a calculation of his pension benefits, and the new actuary reports them as $1 million a year, not knowing that the executive was on a special contract entitling him to only $600,000 a year, this inaccuracy can reflect badly on both the new actuary and on the internal administrator. Therefore, given the complexity of the pension system, the administrator will likely prefer to stay with the old actuary who already understands it.

Financial people, particularly a chief financial officer, are also cautious about changing actuaries. They seldom understand what an actuary actually does, but they need financial information related to pensions, and it must be accurate and on time. Inadequate information can cause extra work, embarrassment, and a loss of confidence in the investment community. As long as the CFO is getting what he needs from the incumbent actuary, he'll have bigger fish to fry and will be unlikely to risk changing actuaries, even if he knows that other firms might do the work better.

For these reasons, an actuary who builds the right relationships with a client's human resources and financial departments will be hard to displace. A similar case can be made for the costs associated with switching many other kinds of professionals.

Because clients are reluctant to incur switching costs, portal projects seldom require the displacement of a current service provider. They will instead address something the current provider isn't dealing with or may not have the skills to handle. Or, they will address an area not covered by the current provider. For example, an organization's current counsel may be conflicted in a specific case, offering another law firm an opportunity to represent a client and demonstrate its expertise. When an accountant offers to review a company's tax liabilities, he is offering a service that doesn't require displacing the current auditor.

They Are Cutting-Edge

One way to offer something not being addressed by an entrenched competitor is to offer something so new that no one else is doing it. This is one reason why intellectual capital development is so important at many leading professional service firms.

An accountant from a large firm was once described as follows:

> He's always had a vision that was ahead of everyone else. For example, years ago he was talking to all the banking clients about turning trust accounts into mutual fund accounts. That is old news now, but he was way ahead of the curve back then. Most of the clients didn't know anything about it, but we were well ahead of everyone on this, and that brought us opportunities.

They Lie at the Intersection of Functional Areas

Another reason why a company may not use another professional or its own staff to address an issue is that the ownership of the issue is unclear. We could say that it "lies at the intersection of two or more functional areas." If these areas both reject responsibility for an issue, or if both claim it, progress can be stalled.

This dilemma provides an opportunity for a professional to come in and work with all the departments involved to proceed around the roadblock. Creating an action plan to resolve such an issue can certainly make a good portal project.

An example of how to operate at the intersection between specialties was provided by Mark Weitzel, a partner at the law firm of Thelen Reid & Priest, which specializes in large infrastructure projects:

> I do a lot of front-end structuring work for business deals. This work is at the intersection of business and legal issues where they blend together. [Clients and I] spend a lot of time at the blackboard brainstorming and putting the pieces together. This is usually at the early part of a deal. Then I turn over the resulting legal work to our partners.
>
> For example, I helped design a company to construct, operate, and improve privatized airports. We had to deal with where the money was coming from and how the governance would be set up. The client needed a way to set up a board with diverse partners that would get the work done and wouldn't let the organization stagnate. There had to be a way for the partners to get their money out of the deal. A lot of different kinds of legal work spun off of these discussions.

They Are Services Your Firm Is Known For

If a firm has a reputation for being one of the premier providers in a particular area, it can sometimes use that service as a portal without discounting its fees. Leading strategy consulting firms, in effect, do this with strategy projects. In some cases, the work they provide in this area can lead to large implementation projects.

The law firm of Hale and Dorr used its reputation in one area to gain access to an account and build its presence from there. Twenty years ago, the firm was well known for its corporate technology practice. Based on this reputation, the founders of one of the original biotechnology companies hired Hale and Dorr to do corporate work. They gave their intellectual property work to another specialist firm.

Five years later, the company ended up in a life-or-death battle with a competitor on an intellectual property issue. Throughout the trial, Mark Borden, the Hale and Dorr attorney in charge of the account, kept the company's general counsel informed of the firm's litigation experience. At one point, he introduced him to Bill Lee, one of the firm's top litigators on intellectual property issues. Two years later, an injunction was filed against the company and the general counsel replaced the attorneys he had been using on the case with Hale and Dorr. The next round of litigation went much more favorably for the client, and Hale and Dorr was eventually given all of the company's intellectual property work.

These are some of the characteristics of portal projects. No portal project is likely to have all of them, but all have some of them. Many firms find that one or two standard portals work in many situations. They carefully craft them to be easy to sell and deliver high value. Such efforts can provide a high return. Exhibit 3.1 provides an exercise that can help you identify a good portal service for your firm.

Exhibit 3.1

Creating a Portal Service

A portal service can help you start relationships with clients and position you for more work. Answering the following questions may help you create such a service for your firm:

Alternatives Generation
- *What has worked in the past?*

    Don't make the problem harder than it need be. If something has worked in the past, there is a good chance it will work again. Look at the first services that clients hire you for and see if they can be redesigned as effective portals.

- *What service could be split out from an existing bundle of services and provided as a portal?*

  Some firms have created effective portals by splitting off a first phase or step in a typical assignment and selling or providing it free to a client.

- *What kinds of diagnostics, evaluations, or workshops do you offer?*

  Most portals take the form of diagnostics, evaluations, or workshops of some kind. If you offer these kinds of services, you should evaluate them to see if you have any that could be provided as a portal.

Alternative Screening

Once you have generated alternative ideas for a portal service, screen them by answering the following questions about each:

- *Does the service provide clear value to the client? Is it something you do really well?*

  To work effectively as a portal, a service must provide clear value to a client and that value must be easy to identify in advance. Unless the client gets obvious value from a portal service, it isn't likely to hire you for additional work.

- *Is it likely to create price resistance? Can the people you know in your client organizations hire you for this work?*

  Price should not create a purchase barrier for most portals. It must be something that can be provided at a modest cost to the person who hires you. Naturally, the price can be higher if you are selling to a CEO than if you are selling to a manager. The people you normally deal with at a client must be able to hire you for this work or you must find a way to sell at another level in the organization.

- *Will the work help you meet people you want to know in the client organization?*

Second only to providing the client with high value, your goal in providing a portal service is to meet key buyers and influencers in the client organization. A portal must be designed to help you do that.

- *Will it require displacing another firm?*

The most effective portals offer services that don't require displacing a competitor.

4

Buyers: The People We Need to Know

Buyers are important because you sell to people, not to accounts. Cross selling, like all sophisticated selling, is based on meeting the right people, developing relationships with them, and understanding their concerns. I have indicated a number of good books that address various aspects of this issue,[1] and I recommend that you seek them out. In this book, we will focus on developing relationships with buyers in order to cross sell and in-sell certain services.

The value of working with buyers in order to cross sell your services can be seen in the following story. It was told to me by Mike Corey, an executive recruiter at TMP Worldwide. TMP provides an array of recruiting services, of which executive search is only one. As you read, notice the portal project, but put your main focus on the buyers.

A friend of mine is the vice-chairman of [a large financial institution]. I have known him for twenty-five years from the days when he worked at [another company]. He would always call me when things weren't going well or when he had staffing issues, but we never talked business in the sense of my asking him to hire us. I go to his golf tournament once a year.

One day he called me and said he was interviewing a person for a job and asked what I thought about him. He also asked if there was anyone out there who might be better. He described the guy, whom I already knew, and I said he was good, but he wasn't the right person to work with him. I know how my friend works; he's creative and disorganized. This candidate was too structured, and wouldn't make a good partner, which was what my friend wanted.

He then asked if I knew other people, and I offered to introduce him to a couple of candidates. We didn't talk fee or business. I later made the introductions, and my friend interviewed them and thought they still weren't right. He asked if I knew anyone else. I said I thought I knew the right guy, and when I told him the name, he already knew him. In fact, this person had worked for him long ago. He agreed that this was the person he wanted, and at that point I offered to put in some more work on this; would he like a search? He said yes. That's the way our business relationship started—very informally.

After I started the work, the new head of human resources called and said he wanted to participate in the negotiations around our fee, so they could put a cap on it. I agreed and went to see him. My friend's company had always used [two other large executive search firms], and I needed a relationship with this HR person because he had access to a lot of other searches. I knew that how I handled the negotiations would influence how he felt about me. We negotiated a fair and equitable arrangement, and that helped him view me as a true professional.

Still, it was only a start. The HR head needed to know things about me that the vice-chairman already knew. So I worked directly with him and treated him as if he were my main contact.

After a lot of hard work, we got the candidate hired, and the HR head felt great about us. The vice chairman was also pleased that his head of HR was happy.

Not long after that the HR head called me with the next big assignment. He referred me to the person on his team in charge of executive recruiting. I then transferred my relationship over to him. The recruiting head had access to all the searches, and when the top HR man left, this chap took his place. Now we do many searches with him each year.

One day I was meeting with him and he happened to say, "I can get anyone to do $1 million searches; everyone wants them. My real problem isn't those half dozen big searches I do a year. My real problem is the 150 openings I have between $75,000 and $150,000 that I don't know what to do with." This was a mix of jobs under the screen of most executive search firms, and in what would normally be the contingency fee area.

I brought in one of our top executives to talk about "executive resourcing," a service that could help him in this area that is distinct from contingency fee work. Later, they called back and said they needed to hire thirty or so people in a specific area. I brought in Laurelle Mathis from our Executive Resourcing unit, and she did a hell of a job for them.

By this time, we knew a lot of people on the client's HR team, and they were true believers in our capabilities. We asked for a chance to talk with some other company leaders who had recruiting needs but whom we hadn't met. These were executive vice presidents (EVPs). The HR people agreed and told the EVPs that it would be worth an hour of their time. (One of these meetings has led to a large, complex assignment requiring several services to recruit several hundred people.)

I have shortened this story a good deal to retain the focus on buyers. If you review it, you will find that they include the vice-chairman, the head of human resources, the head of executive recruiting who was later promoted to the top HR position, several other HR people, and several executive vice presidents. There are almost certainly others not mentioned. The deep relationship that Corey and TMP Worldwide have with the company is really, of course, the result of these relationships, all of which were essential to cross-selling success.

The Whole Is Worth More Than the Sum of the Parts

Our research into cross selling shows that if you have many relationships with a given client, the whole is worth more than the sum of the parts.[2] This is because the more people you talk with at an account, the more combinations of information you can make. These combinations will allow you to better determine how you may increase your value to the client and to identify more cross-selling opportunities for the client. As Exhibit 4.1 shows, the number of combinations of information you can make grows geometrically with the number of people you talk to in an account. If you talk with fifty people in an account, you're in a far stronger position to draw more inferences than if you talk to only two.

This is because talking with many people at an account provides consistent value by giving you information that eases all your conversations at the company. You can often give information you get from A to B and vice versa. Statisticians call these potential flows of information "permutations." As can be seen in Exhibit 4.1, the number of permutations grows even faster than combinations do, as your network of contacts grows in an account.

The exhibit shows why knowing many people at a client increases your effectiveness there. The information flows at your disposal (represented by lines) grow geometrically with the number of people (represented by circles) that you know at the client. As the number of people (N) doubles from three to six to twelve, the number of one-way flows (C for combinations) grows much faster. The number of two-way flows (P for permutations, giving information from A to B and B to A) grows faster still.

Take the case of Alan Weyl, a partner at CSC Consulting, when he was working for a large telecommunications equipment manufacturer. During the course of the work, Weyl and his team talked with people in many areas of the organization. Two mid-level engineers in two different divisions described problems their divisions were having managing order fulfillment and inventories. They needed to lower costs and improve service to key customers in some specific ways.

Exhibit 4.1
The Power of Many Relationships

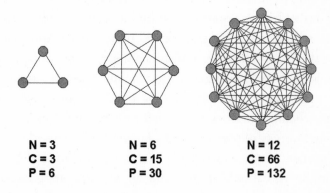

N = 3	N = 6	N = 12
C = 3	C = 15	C = 66
P = 6	P = 30	P = 132

Source: Harding & Company

Yet no one in the company seemed to be aware that the two divisions were facing identical problems. This insight ultimately led to a major sale for CSC. If Weyl and his team hadn't met with so many people in the organization, they wouldn't have been able to gain the insight that showed them how to provide their client with such great value.

In another case, a professional who developed many accounts over a long career, kept a list of everyone he knew at each account in a little notebook. When he had a meeting at an account, he would arrive early and stop in to make brief visits to other people he knew at the site. I once spoke to a young colleague of his who accompanied him on such a visit. The colleague noted in amazement, "By the third meeting, John was passing on information that he hadn't known when he walked in the door." John wasn't passing on anything that was secret; he simply realized that information flows are imperfect in large organizations. John was helping people by improving the flow of information.

Of course, the kinds of information you are likely to access depends on the kinds of people you know at an account. If you know only those members of the general counsel's staff who deal with labor and employment matters, then you are unlikely to get the information you need to sell legal services on environmental matters. If you deal only with people in distribution, you are unlikely to learn how to sell a merchandising consulting project. If you know only the people working at the client's St. Louis site, you are unlikely to pick up projects at its Los Angeles, Atlanta, and Glasgow sites. In the story that began this chapter, one of TMP's major breakthroughs with the client came when Corey met with executive vice presidents running a variety of business units. He was thus exposed to a wide array of client needs, which led to a large assignment for TMP.

Finally, you should understand broad corporate issues when selling services to an organization, which you can only learn about by talking with people in the company. By doing so, you'll gain a depth of understanding vital to your ability to cross sell.

As Frank Ruotolo, who at the time of the interview worked at Deloitte Consulting, says, "It is very important to find out about the power plays and fears and subplots that are going on. Management of a company is made up of many personalities with personal and professional motivations. If you can figure out how these play out, you are way ahead of the game."

At one account, he interviewed many people to gather information needed to prepare a proposal. These people told him many valuable things about their company. For example, two of the senior executives were at loggerheads with each other. One was seen as a delayer, and was committed to keeping the company independent. This kind of information helped Deloitte beat out a competitor for the first assignment, and was valuable throughout the entire relationship with the client as more projects were sold.

That story compares favorably to one told us by a rainmaker at a large accounting firm:

> The biggest obstacle to cross selling we have is not knowing enough about the clients and their needs. We all know our own stuff and can talk about it, but we don't always know enough about the client.
>
> Our audit guys did a presentation at [a large telecommunications company] and did a fantastic job with a very creative video presentation. But there was no message for the client about why he should hire us. That's because they didn't know that going after big clients requires knowing more about the clients themselves.

And that knowledge comes from people you meet in the client's organization. A well-developed account also means that you know most of the buyers even before opportunities arise. Says an accountant, "At one company I work with, if there are five people making a decision on who to hire, we will know four of the them before the issue even comes up."

Knowing a lot of people in an account will obviously help you get business. *Getting to know them* takes a lot of hard work and some ingenuity. This chapter focuses on *who* you need to know and the nature of these new relationships. Later chapters will provide guidance on how to meet the right people.

First, Dance with the One Who Brought You

Relationships can only be developed one a time, starting with your first sponsor. You have to "dance" with the person who brought you, whether or not this is someone with whom you want to have a long-term relationship. Whoever gave you that first key assignment needs to be assured that you do quality work, and that you care about his or her personal success.

Dennis Sullivan, CEO of the consulting firm Robert E. Nolan & Company, says:

We want our sponsor to see that he or she is important to us. Sometimes the sponsor is a vice president, who is used to a larger firm coming in and wanting to meet the president. If I am managing the account, I will be in every two weeks to discuss the project, and to provide additional value by sharing what other companies are doing. That way we deepen our relationship with the key decision-maker on the project. Of course, there are other people we want to get to know, but we don't rush to get to meet them. Step one is to demonstrate to the person who hired you early success on the project for which you were hired.

Sometimes, the person who hired you wants you to work with someone else lower in the organization. Then, it's important that your new contact feels he or she is getting your full attention. Attorney David Harris of Lowenstein Sandler PC says:

Sometimes the top person [in the general counsel's office] decides which outside counsel to hire but expects the lawyers on his staff to actually work on the cases. In most organizations there are people who that top person trusts, and in many matters he or she ceases to be involved. I try to make sure the top person knows who I am, and then focus on making the people who report to him or her look good. I also try to help them satisfy their inside clients. If their inside clients are unhappy, their lives are more difficult. If their inside clients are happy with the work being done, their lives are better.

The same pattern can be seen on large architectural projects. Says Guy Geier of NBBJ:

The real estate or facilities management executive usually initiates a relationship. They issue requests for qualifications and requests for proposals, and then decide if you get short-listed. You make your initial pitch to them. Once a project starts, though, you are likely to spend most of your time with the project level guys. They are the ones who say that you did a good job, thus opening opportunities for other work. You have to keep them happy.

You must have patience to cross sell, and that involves putting in time to take care of the people who hire you, and those to whom you are assigned. Only after they have seen good results can you make a deliberate effort to sell to others.

Look for Sponsors and for People Who Are Predisposed to Be Helpful

A sponsor is someone who wants you to get hired. Therefore, you should always be looking for sponsors. Again and again, the people we interviewed mentioned their importance:

- I wouldn't have stuck to [the long pursuit of an account] if I hadn't trusted that Ken was on our side and would try to get us something.
- After that I knew we had a sponsor and would likely get more work.

Sponsors are a subset of a large category of people—those predisposed to be helpful. It is always worth the effort to develop a relationship with such people. This lesson was taught to me by the late Bruce McNaughton, an extraordinary sales trainer, many years ago. Almost anyone who is predisposed to be helpful is worth knowing, regardless of his or her position. Those that are may be that way because:

- They were brought up to be helpful to others.
- They see opportunities more than others do, and view you as one.
- They are secure and willing to take risks to help others.
- They feel important when helping others.
- They are intellectually curious.
- They simply like you.

In one case, an operations consultant made friends with an advertising vice president at an insurance company. Even though his firm was unlikely to work with the client's advertising department, the consultant developed the relationship, realizing that the man had a generous nature. In time, this vice president introduced the consultant to several people at the company, who later hired him.

Seek Introductions to Cross-functional Buyers

Cross-functional buyers deal with broad business problems that require a variety of disciplines to solve. This might be a merger that requires many services to implement and integrate, or a company's entry into a new line of business. Because they deal with major issues that tend to require cross-functional and cross-geographic solutions, these buyers can help your cross-selling efforts.

Who belongs in this category? It depends on the nature of your profession. For consultants, cross-functional buyers often include CEOs, CFOs, presidents, and business unit heads. For an attorney, it is often the general counsel. For architects and engineers, it is usually the top facilities or real estate person.

If a cross-functional buyer did not hire you for your initial project, chances are you began your business relationship working with people below the cross-functional level. If so, moving up to that level can risk alienating your present contact. We will discuss this issue in greater detail later.

Look for Bridges

"Bridges" is a term devised by Dennis Sullivan, of the consulting firm Robert E. Nolan & Company, to describe people who work in many parts of an account and so are in a position to introduce you to people in different vertical business units. Bridges often work in staff functions, like human resources or information technology. In the story with which this chapter began, Mike Corey used his contacts in the client's human resources department to gain introductions to executive vice presidents of several vertical units.

Although your regular staff contacts are most likely to serve as bridges, anyone who is politically savvy, has influence, and is predisposed to help you develop new business can be considered a bridge.

Build Relationships with Functional Buyers

A "functional buyer" is the person in charge of a specific narrow area. For example, a benefits redesign project may be sold to the benefits manager, an upgrade of a heating system to a facilities engineer, an insurance defense to a low-level attorney within the general counsel's office. When making such a sale, you definitely will need the functional buyer on your side.

Even when you are selling a mix of services to a cross-functional buyer needed to solve a large, complex problem, it helps to have the support of the functional specialists. If they don't like you, they can block your efforts to get hired. Senior executives know that fixing a problem will be much easier if those people responsible for a function approve of the professional hired to help.

As the ex-CEO of a large corporation once told a group of professionals, "I was happy to make introductions for you guys because I knew how good you were. But once I introduced you to the people in my organization, I was reluctant to push you on them. I wanted the people who worked for me to make their own decisions."

Get to the Right Level of Buyer for the Service You Wish to Sell

Once you know that a client needs a service you offer, your job is to get to the person or people who can hire you. This can require you to move either up or down in the client organization, depending on the nature of the need.

This is what Bob Borsch of PricewaterhouseCoopers did when a partner brought him in to meet with the CFO at one of his accounts. The CFO was looking for ways to cut costs, and Borsch soon realized that the CFO could not serve as the sole sponsor for the project. He dealt with this concern directly.

I extracted an agreement from the CFO that I would get a series of meetings with the top-level executives or I wouldn't do the [portal project]. I said that in order to get the costs out of the business and to have the money that was saved redeployed into the right places, the executive group had to be engaged. What we could do would depend on how much they wanted to do, where they wanted to go, and where they were going to get the money to do it. I forced the right expectations and drove the transaction to the right level immediately. It is far too late to do that after you have been working with the client for a while.

But don't assume that you always need to sell at the top levels of the client organization. Borsch was dealing with an issue that needed executive committee attention. That isn't always the case.

As one accountant put it, "It depends on what you are selling. Some things are bought by buyers at midlevel in the organization. High-end buyers need to deal with things that are earth-shattering."

If the issue you have raised isn't earth-shattering, be prepared to sell at midlevels in the client company.

And a lot of good work is authorized at lower levels. One firm spent almost two years with little luck trying to develop relationships with the top officers at a large financial institution. These officers already had relationships with other professionals and weren't interested in getting to know new ones.

When the firm changed its focus to business from middle management, it quickly made progress. Within a year, it was doing $5 million worth of work and was working in a number of departments. With that size of a working relationship, the account team leaders now had good reason to go back to the top officers and talk about new projects at a higher level.

Catch Rising Stars

A "rising star" is a capable young person on the way up in an organization. You'll do well to identify these people and start developing relationships with them now. Once they reach positions of power, all your competitors will be vying for time with them. The professional who knew them before they reached a higher position will have an edge when it comes to business. And, as these rising stars' careers develop, they can take you with them to other parts of their organizations or to new and interesting kinds of work.

For example, a lawyer had worked on a series of employment discrimination cases for a client but had not been able to gain other kinds of work for his firm. He relates:

The attorney who was head of the labor and employment group at this client kept getting promoted, and when he did, he would get involved in broader issues. He finally brought me into an intellectual property matter relating to trade secrets. That was our breakthrough! This project was big, complicated, and extremely important to the company—of concern to the highest levels.

Many professionals lose touch with rising stars when they are transferred to an area outside their expertise. But these people may be able to help them later in their careers or to help cross sell work now. As Hollace Cohen of the law firm Jenkins & Gilchrist says, "When a client moves on to a new area, a lot of lawyers will say, 'Oh well, there will be other work.' They don't see the move as an opportunity to provide work for others in the firm with experience in the client's new area." Responsibility for developing relationships with rising stars can be assigned to junior people in your firm who are on the way up.

We sell to people, not companies. If we know enough buyers and the right buyers in the companies we are targeting, the chances of selling additional work increase. It helps to know a mix of people—cross-functional buyers, bridges, and functional buyers—but above all, people who are predisposed to be helpful. Of course, we have to find ways to meet buyers and then to develop relationships with them. This is covered in the next chapter.

5

Events: How You Drive the Process

Events create opportunities for you to talk with buyers about their concerns. They offer both time and common experiences—two key ways to develop relationships with people you want to get to know.

Events are important because they can be scheduled. You can monitor your progress by keeping track of the number of events you can hold or attend with sought-after buyers. The more events you can schedule with the right buyers, the better chance that you will sell more work. No events, no progress.

The following quote by Les Sherman, an attorney at Thelen Reid & Priest's San Francisco office, reveals how he views the process of building relationships with buyers through events.

Get to know as many people in a client's organization as you can. I've found that it can be awkward and difficult to follow up with someone after a deal closes because they are likely to think you are just looking for work. The better the relationship, the easier this is. It's critical to use the time when you are working with someone to solidify the relationship so that it is easier to call later.

Many of the people I work with are roughly my own age, and it's easy to hang out with them after a meeting for a few minutes and talk. This keeps you in their minds, so that they may call you when they have a legal matter.

We're having our firm's Christmas party the day after tomorrow. That same night, I am invited to a dinner to celebrate a closing. I'm going to the dinner because it's a chance to get to know these clients better in a social setting. I also go to certain clients' Christmas parties.

I do a lot of international work, which requires considerable travel. That provides time during which you can get to know a client and become a friend. For example, this past week I was on a flight to Asia with the senior business person in a client company. Once there, we had meals together, which helped to solidify our bond.

While visiting [the U.S. headquarters of a manufacturing client] on a legal matter, I asked my client for something with the company's name on it, like a cup or a cap. He took me down to an area near the human resources department, and I used this opportunity to ask for an introduction to someone in the department. He introduced me to the head of HR, and now we are doing labor work for them.

Once again, I have shortened the story, but the message is clear: Sherman, like all the professionals interviewed for this book, uses events to meet and develop relationships with buyers. In his story, you can find many kinds of events used this way: client meetings, informal visits, a closing dinner, Christmas parties, airplane trips, and dinners with a client while traveling.

Again and again, the professionals we interviewed emphasized the importance of spending time with clients. Said Mike Palmer, a founder and partner at the consulting firm DiamondCluster, "It's sort of like raising children. You need quality time with a client, but you need quantity time, too. If I'm not at [a major investment banking firm] for a couple of weeks, [my primary contact] will figure out another way to get things done."

Steve Vernon, an actuary with Watson Wyatt Worldwide put it this way, "See the client and business will come." Another professional said, "When you spend time with clients, good things tend to happen." All these quotes describe the continuing need for face-to-face contact.

Books on selling don't usually discuss events, probably because most books are written for dedicated sales forces whose primary job is to make sales calls. Because dedicated salespeople don't do client work, they lack access to many of the events available to professionals. Whatever the reason, events are a rarely explored—but vitally important—topic.

There are two kinds of events. The first kind arises as a part of the work you are doing for your client. Whenever you meet with clients, some of those meetings will be potential cross-selling events.

When I use the term "cross selling" here, I am not referring to a *hard* sale. I mean meeting people, developing relationships, flagging issues for later discussion, and the myriad of other small details that put you in a strong position to make a sale when a client mentions a need.

In addition, I am referring to what happens both during the meeting and while you wait in the room before the meeting, during breaks, and just after the meeting breaks up. Some professionals view these moments as "downtime," but rainmakers know these all present opportunities to talk with people.

Those who are effective at cross selling, and those who are not, differ in the way they handle events that are a normal part of their work with clients. Les Sherman also speaks to this issue: "I have two goals when I talk with a client: The first is to solve his problem, and the second is to make him want to call me again. Too often, people focus exclusively on the first of these goals."

The kinds of events that occur as a part of normal client work will differ from profession to profession, and from firm to firm, and even from specialty to specialty. Some professions, like management consulting, have distinct titles for most of the events that are part of their work.

Though there are obvious advantages to meeting with clients at events that are required to complete an assignment, sometimes you just can't get to someone you want to meet this way. You must then use an event that is not part of any specific assignment, such as a golf outing or a professional association meeting. Professionals use such events both to meet people at an account they are trying to land and to develop existing relationships.

The major categories of events are described in detail on the following pages. Exhibit 5.1 provides a listing of events for quick reference later.

Exhibit 5.1

Events Checklist

Relationships are begun and developed at meetings. Meetings with buyers are also the best places to identify signals that a client may need additional services and to increase the client's commitment to using you to provide those services. Review this checklist when you need to meet with a buyer but are unsure how. It summarizes the most common kinds of events available to you.

Event	*Description*
Fact Finding	A meeting to learn about the client's issues and needs. Can be a part of a larger service or larger sales process. These are a good place to start or further develop a relationship and to identify signals from clients for more needed services.

Update and Review	A meeting to inform the client about recently completed work and plans for coming weeks, and to receive the client's feedback.
Strategizing and Planning	A meeting to determine a course of action, weighing its strengths and weaknesses.
Idea Generation and Consensus Building	A meeting to generate ideas by brainstorming (or some other technique) or to obtain a group's commitment to a course of action.
Negotiating	A meeting to negotiate something on behalf of the client. The client must be present for this kind of event if it is to help you with cross selling.
Travel	A trip with a client to conduct a site visit, interview people, or negotiate with them as required by the work you have been hired to do.
Client Education	A meeting or workshop to inform clients about something they would benefit from knowing.
Celebrations	An event marking the successful completion of a major task.
Drop-Bys	A casual meeting with a client made simply because you are going to be in the area on other business.
Sales	Meetings to advance or make a sale. These can be initiated either by you or by the client. They range from cold calls to introducing yourself and your services to responding to a client's request for help with a specific issue.
Social and Service	A gathering to have fun or to make a social contribution.
Professional	An association meeting to stay abreast of issues of importance to a profession or industry and to network.

Fact-Finding Meetings

All professionals meet with representatives of client organizations to learn the specifics about the assignment they have been hired to complete. These meetings go by a variety of names; for example, architects have programming meetings, consultants have project interviews, litigators have depositions and meetings that prepare for depositions. They all provide crucial input into the professionals' later work.

Because it is your job to learn at such meetings, you have an excellent opportunity to meet people in the client organization, learn about their concerns, and develop a relationship. These are good places to flag new issues that may bring in more work for your firm later. Professionals who are good at cross selling will eagerly take full advantage of these opportunities. As one such professional put it:

> The people in a client organization can be broadly fit into three groups. First, there are those you have to meet with to learn what you need to know to do your work. Of course, you meet with them. Second, there are those it would make no sense to meet with, and of course, you don't waste their time by meeting with them. But there is a third group that falls somewhere between these two. These people are not considered essential for you to meet with, but your work would probably be better if you did. Often, this group gets cut out for budgetary or scheduling reasons. But if these people might hire you for more work, you should absolutely meet with them. Usually, meetings can be scheduled with this third group if you simply ask for them.

Many professionals are straightforward with their clients about the value of such meetings. A tax partner at a large accounting firm was hired to do an assessment that would require interviews with many people at the client company. He told his contact that he would also be bringing other partners from his firm with him to some of the meetings. First, they had content knowledge that would be of value to the meetings. Second, the partner wanted his client's people to see the resources his firm could bring to bear on their issues. His contact responded, "Good idea!"

I have worked with hundreds of professionals to help them figure ways to meet a potential executive client. They are usually willing to pay good money in travel expenses or seminar costs to obtain a meeting. In the process, however, I sometimes learn that they actually passed up an opportunity to meet this very executive in a fact finding meeting for work they had previously done at the client organization. You can avoid losing such opportunities if you always consider the long-term relationships you want to build while completing your work with a client.

As we have seen, a good portal project can provide an opportunity for extensive fact finding. Firms that have penetrated an account deeply have almost always done a considerable amount of factfinding there.

Sales meetings may, at times, be almost indistinguishable from fact finding meetings. Indeed, during the sales process, smart professionals request fact finding interviews whenever they can. In such cases, the sales process itself can serve as a portal project.

Update and Review Meetings

All professionals will meet with the client for updates and review meetings where they brief a client on the progress of the work they are doing, resolve outstanding issues, and make tactical plans for moving ahead. Also known as project meetings and client briefings, they provide excellent opportunities for you to demonstrate your professionalism, earn trust, and learn about other situations in the client organization that may affect your work.

These meetings can be held at several levels, including meetings with the client's project or case manager, meetings with a project task force, or executive briefings, all with different levels of people in the client organization.

Account development pros use these opportunities, just as they use fact-finding meetings, to meet people in the account, develop relationships, and earn trust. If there is to be a project task force, for example, they may be able to influence who will attend it. The same applies to executives invited to attend executive briefings. Rainmakers also use these meetings to elicit "signals," a subject we will deal with in greater detail in the next chapter.

A management consultant told this story about how he obtained one-on-one briefings with a client, the CEO of a large corporation:

> We had been retained for our first assignment with this company and saw it as a big opportunity. But our first monthly review with the management committee was a disaster. It was the kind of meeting that causes nightmares. We would say that based on what we had learned, the first priority was to do X, but a member of the management committee would say, "No, it's not." We would say that we think you should do Y, and someone would say, "No, we won't." So it went for a miserable hour and a half.
>
> At the end of the meeting I went up to the CEO and said that this meeting was a travesty for both of our organizations, and that he and I couldn't let it happen again. To avoid future problems, I recommended that he and I meet one-on-one before each monthly management committee meeting to get in sync with each other. He readily agreed. So now I'm meeting with him twice a month!

In fact, the firm not only salvaged the project after a troubled start, it also did such a good job the client became one of the firm's best accounts for several years.

Let's examine why this consultant's recommendation was the right thing to do from every perspective. First, it was the right thing to do to get the initial project back on track. Second, it was the right thing to do from a marketing perspective. The discussions between the consultant and the CEO, and the relationship they developed during their one-on-one meetings, were key to the consultant's ability to win many future assignments.

Regular review meetings are a wise practice whenever you have a large, complex relationship with a client. David Nash, an engineer with Parsons Brinckerhoff, is working on a site redevelopment for a manufacturer. When completed, the project will affect six million square feet of building and involve 35,000 moves of personnel over five or six years. The firm's work involves numerous projects, each of which requires their meeting with the client. But Nash also needed to manage the overall client relationship.

> I sat down with the client quarterly to talk about how we were doing. We began these meetings to give the client a chance to step back from daily management and reflect on how we were doing in a holistic manner. We talked about how specific aspects of our service applied to the total program we were helping them manage. They talked about what we were doing well and what could be done better. Even though we met daily on the individual projects, it's helpful to do this formally to look at broader issues. I started each meeting by saying, "This is what you were concerned about last time; how is it going now?" Then I would say, "Here are things we are thinking of doing. What do you think of these ideas?"

The firm started this relationship with one small job. Now it is working on its twenty-second project!

Clients sometimes ask for review meetings, anticipating getting added value. One manager at a telecommunications company told a human resources consultant that they wanted regular reviews.

So we schedule a monthly phone call to go over all the things we are doing for them around the world and how it is all going. I am also expected to tell them things we see that they need to know about. They use us to understand what is going on around the world in their organization as well as any trends and issues they need to be thinking about.

These monthly phone meetings provide value to the client. It doesn't take much imagination to recognize that they are also great selling opportunities for the human resources consultant.

Strategizing and Planning Meetings

When it's important to map out alternatives and set directions for future work, these meetings will help to reveal issues that the client needs to have resolved, as well as to provide opportunities for more work. An obvious time to examine these issues is during a kick-off meeting. During these meetings, the client will name your contact people. Listen closely for the reasons the client gives for each referral, as they often reveal issues that are challenging the client.

Lawyers often have such meetings with clients when they have been hired to help with a deal or a lawsuit. Here, a lawyer explains the cross-selling value of these kinds of meetings.

If you're working on an acquisition, a lot of due diligence is required before the deal is sealed. Due diligence is work done to make sure that facts the company to be acquired presents are accurate and complete. Getting involved with the due diligence team is a key way to cross sell. If you are on the team, you can help prepare the due diligence memo, which incorporates all the possible tasks that could affect the execution of your firm's services. That provides you the opportunity to suggest that you can help in different areas, and is a great way to cross sell. We always ask if the client would like us to help generate the memo and, whenever possible, put an associate lawyer from our firm in charge of keeping track of the due diligence checklist so we can see what's been done and what hasn't.

Idea-Generating and Consensus-Building Meetings

Some professional services may require idea-generation and consensus-building meetings. These would include brainstorming sessions and some client workshops. On architectural projects, they include "charettes," or brainstorming sessions to generate design ideas.

IDEO, a top product design firm based in Palo Alto, runs many of these sessions,[1] which are good places to meet people from client organizations, and to identify possible future work. When a European fashion house decided to open a New York flagship store, management wanted the store to make a special statement. Part of it was to be made by new uses of technology, so the architect and the client asked IDEO for help in this area.

At two lengthy brainstorming sessions, one in London and the other in the Netherlands, several ideas surfaced that could put the new store at the cutting edge of retail technology. One idea was to create a changing room with a delayed-playback camera system that let customers see themselves from all directions in the clothes they were trying on.

Says Martin Hoenle of IDEO, "These sessions gave us a lot of direct contact with the client. We worked hard to make sure that the right people from the client would be there." The sessions led to several assignments needed to design and deliver the new changing room and other products.

Negotiating Meetings

Professionals and their clients may meet with third parties to help with negotiations. For example, corporate lawyers help negotiate contracts. An information technology company may help clients negotiate with hardware and software providers.

Travel

Many professionals travel with their clients. These trips can provide excellent opportunities for advancing relationships. Lawyers may travel with their clients to negotiate with third parties. Consultants may travel with clients for many reasons, such as checking out how another company has solved a problem similar to the one that the client is facing. Architects may travel with their clients to help pick out fixtures or key construction materials, such as marble or tile.

Architect Bill Gustafson makes a point of traveling with clients.

> Once we've won a project, we identify buildings that had issues similar to those the client is facing and we go out together to visit them. When we designed a new sciences building for a college in Michigan, the dean of sciences, the vice president of administration, the head of the facilities department, and several others came with us to see similar buildings in Minnesota and Iowa. This helped us create a better design because in the end, when you produce a building, your client has to like it. By traveling with them, you get a better idea of their probable reaction to different ideas. It's also a terrific way to get to know the client and for them to get to know you. This helps you when you attempt to sell more work.

Client Education Meetings

Sometimes, a meeting is held strictly to educate a client on an issue that his or her organization is facing. These are excellent opportunities to demonstrate a firm's additional capabilities. A story by Stephen Quinn of the engineering firm HNTB demonstrates this point. The firm was designing a line extension for a metropolitan rapid transit system.

> Part of our strategy [for penetrating the account] was to use our current project as a reason to interact with people who would be buyers on the next project. We don't like to wait for the request for proposal to come out to get to know people. That's a sure way to lose business.
>
> From public sources, we knew that our client had a seismic retrofitting project coming up, so we made a presentation on the latest seismic technology and how it applied to the structure we were designing. We made this presentation to the people who had hired us for the line extension project, as well as people whom we knew would be buyers in the later seismic retrofit project. We told the client that they had helped develop the seismic criteria we were using and that we wanted to show how these were being implemented in our design. They welcomed the presentation.

Client education meetings can be less formal. Mark Weitzel, a partner at Thelen Reid & Priest, uses this approach with a client who doesn't like to be "sold."

> A client's current legal need is a great opportunity to cross sell in a low-key way. The general counsel at a company we work with isn't interested if I suggest lunch with our antitrust lawyer when he's in town. She is much more interested in someone who can help solve problems now. She calls and says they are making an acquisition in New York, and I suggest that she get a quick update on New York labor issues, and give the name of a partner in our New York office who really knows the New York labor union environment. Virtually all of our practice groups work for this client as a result of such introductions.

Many firms offer seminars on subjects of interest to clients and prospective clients. These serve two purposes: they provide valuable information to clients, and offer the professionals an opportunity to show their expertise and impress the client.

Bill Fredericks, an accounting partner at Deloitte & Touche, developed an initial relationship with the controller of a utility company at a firm-sponsored seminar. He stuck close to this contact during the seminar and followed up with him frequently. Through that relationship he was able to sell significant work to what would eventually become a major account.

Celebrations

Celebrations are customary at key points in some professional projects. The closing dinner after completing a merger or acquisition is one example that we saw in the quote at the beginning of this chapter. Architectural and engineering projects typically have several celebrations, including ground-breakings, topping-off ceremonies, dedications, and openings. These are quasi-social events that can enable you to develop personal relationships with clients.

Drop-Bys

When you are visiting a client for work you are doing, you can often drop by the offices of people you know for a brief visit. Rainmakers make extensive use of this approach. At these impromptu meetings, clients sometimes bring up things that they wouldn't ordinarily call you about. These spontaneous discussions can open up new opportunities for work.

One consultant we were coaching on client development told us that he wouldn't have time to spend on the phone developing relationships because he would be busy with clients over the coming week. On Monday, he would be in Boston, on Tuesday in Detroit, on Wednesday in Memphis, and so on. We suggested he drop by and see one or two people he knew, but wasn't scheduled to meet, at each client location. One of these visits resulted in a $200,000 project with potential to convert to a million-dollar project—all because he stuck his head in to say hello to an old friend!

Of course, if you are near the client's office while on another job, you can always drop by even when there is no current assignment.

Sales Meetings

Sometimes a sales meeting may be your first introduction to a client. Rainmakers recognize that they have two objectives at such meetings: to make the sale and to establish relationships to ease selling there later.

It is wise to take the long view with large accounts because they will need services for years to come. If the time isn't right, back away. Mike Peters, at the time of the interview a partner with PricewaterhouseCoopers, stressed this point.

> When you first meet with a client, you need to focus on being as helpful as you can. That is the foundation of your relationship. If the issue the client is facing isn't appropriate for you, walk away from it and refer the client to a competitor. That shows you have the client's best interests at heart, and helps you get invited back again.

Social and Service Events

Meals, golf outings, professionals sports events, and evenings at the symphony or the theater are just some of the social events that can help professionals develop relationships with clients. Charity events are another opportunity. Many professionals volunteer at charitable, cultural, or religious organizations both for the personal rewards that come from contributing to a worthy cause and to develop relationships with clients.

Still, the most common kind of social event is a business breakfast or lunch, heavily used by people who cross sell. Anita

Hotchkiss, an attorney with Porzio Bromberg & Newman, tells of such a lunch.

> I knew one of the in-house attorneys from a product liability case I had tried for her. When her company was acquired she was moved to the employment law section of the general counsel's office.
>
> I invited her to lunch and said I would bring one of my partners with me. This person had tried a lot of employment cases, but I didn't advertise that. We all talked, and after we had chatted about a variety of topics, the client asked my colleague what she did. That gave us the opportunity to talk about some recent successes we had had on employment matters. The lawyer needed some advice on employment litigation, and we ended up handling it for the client.

Professional Events

Professional and trade association meetings are excellent opportunities to develop and maintain client relationships. Just by attending the right meetings, you can make new contacts and use new opportunities creatively. An accountant told us this story:

> I had met a person at [a client] whom I liked and who seemed like a good contact, so I invited him to speak at [a professional meeting] in Phoenix. After the speech, we played a little golf. He was very appreciative, and the following week he called me and told me he suggested us to their attorney for a litigation support project. The moral of this story is that relationship building is very important. It's the best way to sell services.

Remember, relationships are built at events. The challenge is to meet with a client often enough to maintain a strong relationship. This usually requires a blend of events. Dan Meiland, chairman and

CEO of the executive search firm of Egon Zehnder International, meets with the CEO of one client six to eight times a year.

> Sometimes it is in conjunction with searches, and sometimes I simply come by to see him. I have been to dinner in his home and saw him in Davos, Switzerland, at a symposium, where we had about an hour together.

Spend time with clients and work will come. But you must take the initiative. To make sure that you spend time with clients, schedule events. These may be events required to complete an assignment, which you can also treat as opportunities to advance a relationship. Or, you may create an opportunity to meet with buyers apart from any specific client work.

One way or another, you must meet with buyers. In large part, you can measure your progress at cross selling by the number of events that bring you together with buyers of your services. The more events on tap, the more likely you are to pick up signals that a client needs another service. "Signals" are the subject of the next chapter.

6

Signals: How We Know a Client May Need More Services

A "signal" is an indication that a client needs a service. Often, you get signals from buyers at events. Although you can sometimes get them from other sources, such as the media, that kind of source is available to everyone. You will have no edge on your competitors if you obtain your information only from public sources.

If you obtain signals directly from a buyer, you can find out about a need earlier and discover more about its nuances and details. The simple act of revealing the need means that the buyer is making a commitment to you. It may be modest or it may be large, but it is better than what your competitors are receiving. If you can supplement this advance information with more from public sources, you will have a distinct advantage over your competitors.

The more events you attend and the more buyers that trust you, the more signals you are likely to receive. Sometimes hearing a signal can help save a relationship you already have. Carl

LoBue, founder of LoBue Associates, tells such a story:

> We had been brought in by the CEO of [one of the largest financial institutions in the United States] to help reduce costs. The work was necessary but not popular, because it caused a certain amount of pain. As a result, some of the people the next level down weren't that supportive of what we were doing.
>
> I heard through the grapevine that the client had hired a search firm to find a replacement for the CEO. I knew that if he left, our work would end, so I talked with the headhunter and referred candidates to him, good people with whom I had worked before. One of these candidates was hired, and we were able to complete our work.

In some cases signals don't come from one buyer but are pieced together with information gleaned from several sources. Gary Cawthorne of Unisys Corporation gives a compelling example:

> We had a long history with [a major insurance company] going back maybe fifteen years. We had supported their agent channel with technology we wanted to own, and we would give our professional services away to that end. This eventually evolved into a variety of technology services, mostly maintenance and help desk work. The account was worth $20 million to $30 million a year.
>
> Eventually, the client went out to bid for all this work, and we lost. We had been focused on servicing the old work and had not been cross selling. Suddenly we had nothing. At that point we had to decide whether to abandon the account or to use what we had learned about them to sell more services. We had fifteen people working there full-time and knew maybe 100 people at the client.
>
> We realized that the work we had done gave us insights into their operations and needs that were different from any perspective

they had internally. We had a view across organizational silos because we understood what underwriting, product marketing, agency management, the property and casualty company, and the life company were all trying to do. Once we showed them the value of our intellectual capital, we could provide the bridge.

I have been on a number of sales calls where our team was meeting with someone in the life insurance area and recognized that his need was similar to a need in the property and casualty area. We realized that the two efforts could piggyback on each other because both would come together at the agent level.

This knowledge allowed us to sell new services to the account. We have since helped them with customer relationship management, with e-commerce, and in a variety of other areas. Today, this company is the largest account in my region.

As this example illustrates, the professional who knows the most people in the client company and spends time with them often gets more work. This is not always the case, however.

A professional has to hear signals when they pass his ears. Earlier, the people at Unisys had not recognized the value of what they were hearing until faced with the loss of the account. A professional must also know when and how to ask a follow-up question to develop a clear signal from a mere hint. Otherwise, more time with more buyers won't necessarily produce more work.

Professionals often miss signals, sometimes due to functional thinking and sometimes due to a lack of simple questioning skills. The bigger the team of people on an account, the greater the chance that someone in a firm is receiving signals—and may be missing them.

We will deal in more detail with how to hear signals in Chapter 7. Before we do that, however, we must make clear what signals are and where they are likely to be found.

There are two categories of signals: macro-signals and micro-signals. Macro-signals are major occurrences at a client that create a need for an array of services. Micro-signals indicate a need for a specific service.

Macro-Signals

Major changes at the clients can signal the need for many professional services. Such changes can include:

- Mergers and acquisitions.
- Major restructurings.
- Major changes in stock price.
- Major changes in growth rate.
- The appointment of a new CEO or management team.
- A major change in regulatory environment.
- A major technological change.
- A major corporate relocation.
- Entry into a new business or market.

The number of specific professional services needed by a company as a result of such changes can be great. Take, for example, the merger of American Airlines and TWA as described in the *Wall Street Journal*.[1] An article on the merger appeared in April 2001, while the merger was still being planned and executed. In it, the company identified an estimated 10,000 projects that needed attention. Though not all of these required help from professionals, many would. The article cited many examples of projects that would need help from a variety of professionals, including accountants, lawyers, management consultants, engineers, and, probably, architects. Among them were:

- Lawyers and actuaries to conduct due diligence on TWA.
- Information technology consultants to help synchronize

the maintenance schedules, provisioning, and reservations systems of the two carriers.

- Interior/industrial designers to redesign aircraft interiors.
- Potentially, real estate brokers, interior designers, and engineers to convert TWA's administrative center.
- Lawyers to help negotiate and draw up contracts for new leases on TWA aircraft.
- Lawyers and actuaries to help with layoffs resulting from the merger.
- Lawyers to help negotiate and prepare new labor contracts and airport leases.
- Environmental consultants to help implement American's environmental response program at TWA facilities.
- Lawyers to switch TWA licenses to American.
- Consultants to help with the integration of administrative functions.

Perhaps outside professionals weren't used for all of these issues, but they were used for many. And there are other issues for which they were used that aren't mentioned in the article.

Because the demands created by such changes are so huge, every effort should be made to recognize well in advance when they might be coming. This means that someone in your organization should monitor media coverage of the client and the client's Web site. You, too, should monitor information you get from your clients for signals. One accountant, for example, uses his access to a client's intranet to identify other firms the client is hiring. A flurry of activity with an investment banker, for example, is a likely signal that a mega expenditure is in the works.

This information must be combined with that gained from conversations with your contacts in the account. All of your firm's professionals working in an account should be trained to listen for macro-signals, including the following:

How are Senior Executives Spending Their Time?

Senior executives spend their time on major issues. When you schedule time with a senior executive, you may learn about other things in the works, as did, David Keyko, a litigator at the law firm Pillsbury Winthrop, when dealing with a European client. He tells the story this way:

[The company's general counsel and I] would meet both in Europe and in the United States to talk about strategy issues. These ranged from whether to take a particular route in the litigation and its chances for success to what the demand would be on corporate resources, such as expenses and the need for senior people to testify. When we talked about the demand on executive time, the conversation would naturally flow into a discussion about what the company was doing. [One of the issues that came up this way was] the company's plans to enter the U.S. market.

The conversation then turned to how the company was going to finance this change. By this time I knew the general counsel fairly well and I felt confident enough to ask him. He described a process which would probably require an American counsel for certain aspects.

Keyko was able to involve a partner from the corporate practice who already knew the account, and the firm got the business.

Bob Krauss, a corporate attorney with Schnader Harrison Segal & Lewis, tells of calling a client on a legal matter. The client didn't have much time to talk because he had to catch a plane to Boston. "So I asked what he would be doing there and learned that the company was thinking of making an acquisition in New England." This information led to work for the firm's Boston office.

What Other Professionals Are Being Hired?

Professionals are often hired to plan and implement change. If it is a major change, the client may need many additional services. If the client has hired an investment banker or a strategy consultant or a top-level executive recruiter, it could be a signal of a major impending change. If the firm has retained a technology consultant, this may signal a change in technology with implications for many other aspects of the client's services. Hiring of a leading real estate broker may indicate a move, and a possible need for many professional services during relocation.

Sales effectiveness consultant David Fritz had been working at a technology company for several years when he learned that the client had hired a well-known strategy consulting firm. The firm was asked to evaluate changes in the structure of the company's major market, and to design an appropriate strategy to deal with the changes.

Although this project postponed the more tactical projects Fritz had hoped to pursue with the client, it also tipped him to a new opportunity. After all, if the client changed its business strategy, it would probably need to reorganize its sales force, too. That knowledge eventually helped him sell a project to redesign the sales force a year later, displacing the strategy firm as supplier.

What Issues Are Stopping or Delaying Work?

When a client stops or delays your work, always ask why and get as much detail as you can. Delays can often signal a major change of some kind. The preceding story about David Fritz provides an example of such a delay.

Who is Changing Jobs?

When someone new is brought in at a senior level in a client organization, that person has a mandate and a desire to make a positive impression. That new arrival can signal many changes.

Ray Manganelli, a partner with the consulting firm SDG, says:

I always look at executive changes at major corporations as a clear buying sign. I follow executive changes in the *Wall Street Journal*, the *New York Times,* and the trade journals of the industries I am interested in. I also look at the help wanted ads, because a company hiring for several mid-level positions may indicate a change afoot.

For example, our firm hadn't worked for a multibillion dollar leasing company for several years. Articles in the business press always referred to the Chief Operating Officer (COO) as the heart and soul of the company. When he was replaced with someone else, I figured the board wanted to make some changes.

We called the CEO, a contact from our previous work for the company, and asked what was going on. He told us about the changes the company was undertaking and introduced us to the new COO. That led to a major assignment to help them with divestitures—a new area for us with this client.

What Doesn't Add Up?

When there is a serious disconnect between what logic dictates and what you actually see at a client, it may signal that the client is confused about meeting a major need. Help the client clarify the issue and you could be on track for a major assignment.

Roger Pratesi, now a partner at The Boston Consulting Group, recalls meeting earlier in his career with the top management of a client that needed to cut costs. He was struck by two oddities. First, the firms he was asked to compete against included a large strategy firm, a technology firm, and a boutique. Second, the assignment under discussion was a need to reduce costs by $5 million, a pittance for such a senior team. These two oddities suggested to him that the client was facing a major cost problem and couldn't get agreement on what to do about it. He was right, and later helped the client clarify its need and reach agreement on a course of action. This resulted in several major assignments leading to savings of over $100 million for the client.

What Do the Financial Analysts Advise the Client To Do, and How Is the Company Responding?

All companies are under pressure from their analysts to do something—either they are making a lot of money and must find ways to use the profits, or they aren't and must fix the problem. Most firms also have to look ahead to ensure that profits will continue to flow in the future. Though corporate leaders may not obey the analysts, they are unlikely to ignore such influential critics. Staying on top of what the analysts are saying and observing the company's response can provide signals about major opportunities.

In addition to encouraging your people to be alert, there are other things you can do to increase awareness of a client's macro-signals. For example, you can list the client's major issues and discuss them with your colleagues working on the account. David Ping, a partner at Kurt Salmon Associates, has his teams create a short list of the next three major issues the client is likely to face. By doing so, he keeps his team members focused on what is important to the client, and on ways that his firm can help.

Micro-Signals

You do not need to wait for a major issue to get work from a client. Many professional services are required to help solve small or purely functional problems. If a client says, "Our incentive system is so messed up, our sales force is focusing on the wrong kinds of sales," you'll probably need to address the sales forces compensation system, not overhaul the whole company. If a client says it will take three weeks to get you information that should be available now, this signals a need for an improved information system. If a client says that customers are complaining about possible health effects of the product, it indicates a potential product liability issue, not a tax matter. All of the above are micro-signals, and should be acted upon once recognized.

If you talk regularly with your clients, you are likely to hear many of these signals every year. But unless you are familiar with the factors that create demand for the many services your firm offers, you could miss them. Here are some ways to ensure that these signals will be recognized.

Make Sure the Right People Meet with the Client

Staffing that makes the most economic sense in terms of a specific job may not make sense if you want to cross sell services. Seasoned sales professionals are more likely to recognize signals than junior people with a more technical outlook. One role of the senior professional is to recognize when an apparently routine assignment really isn't, and to staff it accordingly.

Muriel Robinette, of the consulting engineering firm Haley & Aldrich, tells this story about turning a portal project into a large account:

> I met the corporate environmental health and safety director from [a large chemical company] at an association meeting. His company was planning to lease out a facility it owned, and he needed a quick walk-through of the property to comply with the closeout of a facility in accordance with RCRA (the Resource Conservation and Recovery Act). At the time, this was merely a checklist item he needed to do to lease the property and was to be done cheaply.
>
> Because of my experience with older facilities, I suspected there might be bigger issues. However, I wasn't going to say anything at this stage because I didn't want to appear to be pushing for more work before I knew the facts. Instead, I would service him with bells and whistles on the routine assignment. That would earn the right to say, "I also observed this. . . ." You need to earn trust to talk that way. I needed to show him that we would do what he asked faster and better than he expected.

Because the work on these little jobs is routine, clients don't expect to get senior staff. But I made sure that I remained personally involved because, in this case, I felt my experience would be worth something extra to the client. I had a field staff person with me who could do the routine part of the work, but I was there to learn more about the company and its issues.

We spent about three hours at the plant, which gave me an opportunity to look around, see things, and talk to people. My eyes were wide open; to me, this was more than simple data gathering.

I noticed that the loading dock, where they loaded and unloaded chemicals, was near the property line and abutted the town water supply. By asking a few questions, I learned that the company had bought the plant a number of years before and had never done an assessment of potential contamination. In fact, they didn't know if there was a contamination problem that could affect groundwater and potentially threaten the water supply.

However, if they were to lease the building, it would be essential to do this, particularly because that would help establish who was responsible if the new tenant created a problem. If a problem already existed, the previous owner might have been responsible. The sooner the assessment was done, the less confusion there would be in establishing that fact. Burying their heads in the sand was not acceptable. The company needed to know the status of the site from both a defensive and an offensive position.

I also noticed a dip tank in the plant. From experience, I knew that it should have been permitted under RCRA, and so I asked if it had been. I got blank stares in return. If a government inspector discovered this oversight, it could lead to fines of $25,000 a day, while getting the permit would cost a fraction of that.

Still, I didn't push these issues. I just suggested that they were things my client might want to look into. I was able to translate technical issues into business issues far better than a simple routine report for compliance could have done. Pretty soon he came back to us and asked us to work on them.

On the basis of the trust Robinette developed from this work, the client became a major account of her firm. Since that first job, Haley & Aldrich has worked for this company in eight states and in Mexico. If it had been the field staff person who had done the walk-through, one or both of the signals might have been missed, and the working association might have remained a $2,000 relationship.

Sometimes more than one senior person is needed. A client approached a management consulting firm to find ways to remove costs of an acquisition it had made. The consultant from the firm we interviewed admitted that in the past they would have simply sold another cost reduction project. But this time he took a technology specialist and a change management specialist with him. These people were able to recognize the client's problem in ways that the lead consultant might not have. As a result, the firm proposed a more comprehensive approach to the problem than it had in the past, which required work from several practices. The client was delighted with the improved approach, and the consultants received a much larger fee.

Says the consultant, "We were called in because of our strength in re-engineering, but the client didn't bat an eye at our bringing in other services. When you have credibility with a client, you need to think about all the ways you can help them."

If you want to pick up signals, you need to have the right people listening and looking.

Train Your People to Recognize When the Client Needs Other Services Your Firm Offers

Everyone working on an account needs to learn how to pick up signals for the major services your firm offers. This subject is so important that much of Chapter 12 is devoted to it.

Pay Attention to What Questions Your Client Is Asking

If a client is asking about something, it's likely to surface later as an issue. Always pay attention to casual requests for information. If you are in charge of an account team, get your team members to tell you what their contacts in the client organization are asking. This can give you a real competitive edge.

The engineering firm Weston & Sampson pursues public sector work that its clients must bid out competitively in most cases. The firm won a supervisory control and data acquisition (SCADA) study for a New England town. Knowing about the opportunity ahead of the competition helped. Says Jack Jolls, who led the pursuit for Weston & Sampson, "We had been working for the town for a long time and knew a SCADA project might be coming months before the request for proposal was issued. The head of the Department of Public Works had asked us about SCADA and we gave him some technical information about it. It just came up as an aside in a project meeting we were having."

Audie Dunham of the accounting and consulting firm RSM McGladrey says, "When a client raises an issue by saying 'I wish I had help with . . .' or 'I know it's not your area, but do you know anything about . . .', it's a signal that should trigger a response."

Gain Access to Events Where Signals Are Likely to Come Out

Signals can emerge at any time and any place, but they are most likely to surface at certain key events. Therefore, it is critical to gain a seat at the table at such events.

In Chapter 5, we saw that when helping a company with an acquisition, a lawyer should serve on the due diligence committee. That's where the client will be discussing all the areas in which it must perform due diligence, including a review of litigation against the target company, a review of potential environmental liabilities, a review of potential pension liabilities, and many other such issues.

Being present at the meeting allows the lawyer to hear a long list of signals for needs for services, as well as how the client plans to address those issues. In time, the lawyer can offer to help.

This is true in other kinds of professional work, too. Joe Buskuhl, the president of HKS Architects, points out that charettes for a site plan are opportunities to obtain numerous signals. A charette, you'll recall, is a brainstorming meeting in which all the concerned parties in a project are brought together in an intensive, short session to generate design concepts. When, for example, a hospital is rethinking how it will use all its facilities, the charette will involve the key players at the institution with an eye to each facility's future need. Not only is this information essential for planning future use of the site, it is also a great list of potential future projects.

But the event you want to attend where signals are likely to surface may not be associated with your work. In such cases, getting an invitation isn't easy. You might want to follow the examples of professionals who have successfully provided the client with a good reason why they should attend.

The public relations firm Bliss Gouverneur & Associates specializes in work for professional firms. Abby Gouverneur Carr was working with a strategy consulting firm to rebuild its image in its market after years of decline. When she learned of the firm's monthly leadership meetings, she asked to attend one.

> We were put on the agenda to present the results of our program. Once there I realized that this was the place where the partners were most likely to showcase their work, share the results of major assignments, and describe new methodologies. We could learn a lot by being the fly on the wall and listening to the partners talk. So we said that if you want us to capture your best thinking, we urge you to invite us to the meetings where your best thinking is being presented.

Those meetings turned out to be the leadership meetings. Using her firm's public relations expertise, she dramatically increased results achieved by the PR program, educated the leadership team on how best to achieve their marketing goals, and helped them take advantage of their best thinking.

Name recognition for the client in the business media increased from last to fourth in a list of twelve competitors in two years. It also increased the quantity of work her firm received. Over four years, the amount of work this client generated grew to three times its original volume.

Do Work That Surfaces Signals

Signals can be heard on any assignment, but some assignments are likely to put you in the path of many signals. These are premium projects to be avidly sought.

The classic example of such an assignment is the financial audit. Most large accounting firms wish their people did a better job of cross selling, but these firms are actually far more successful than most. Why? Because audit work generates many signals that the firms can then address with other services.

Arthur Andersen was a leader in this approach. From the day he bought and renamed his accounting firm, he pushed his people to promote a broad array of services. He recognized that auditors knew many things about each company they serviced and felt that his firm would be remiss if it didn't bring important issues to their attention. Andersen invented the management letter, which accompanied each audit and listed things that management should consider. Andersen believed that this letter should be so packed with valuable information that it was worth the cost of the audit. The letter was, of course, built around signals picked up during the audit. Management letters are now common practice in the industry.[2]

Firm managers should seek out opportunities to do the kinds of jobs that are likely to surface a large number of signals.

Ask What's Coming

It is also possible to simply ask for signals. If you have a close relationship with a client and that client wants to continue working with you, you can certainly ask about future plans. This is in the client's best interests as well as yours because you want to have the right resources available as they are needed. Early warning gives you the chance to put those resources in place.

Many of the professionals we interviewed already do this with their best clients. Says management consultant Mike Palmer of his relationship with one client:

> I always ask her what's keeping her up at night and what new projects are coming down the line that we should be thinking about. We have a very open professional relationship. In fact, we are at the point where we haven't written a proposal there for over two years. We have a master services contract and write arrangement letters. Terms are negotiated in advance, so that when a project comes along, we are ready to go.

> When the relationship is this close, it is just good business to ask what the client will want you to do next.

> To cross sell you need to know buyers. Events are a good place to get to know them. You will also need to obtain signals from buyers about their future plans, and most signals are given at events. Rainmakers flag signals from a client and bring the issues up in event after event until the client is ready to discuss them. Of course, certain techniques are effective to obtain events and to surface signals. These techniques are the subject of the next chapter.

7

Techniques: Tools for Making It Happen

Professionals use techniques to obtain events with buyers, to elicit signals, and to increase a client's commitment to acting on an issue. Skill at using these techniques makes a professional effective at cross selling, because professionals use techniques to manage the other three elements of the BEST Selling Model: buyers, events, and signals.

The term *sales technique* may connote manipulation to some, but that is not how I think of it. None of the techniques reported by the rainmakers we interviewed were devious or underhanded; most were extremely straightforward.

Take this example told by Milton Smith, now with HNTB, but at the time with another firm:

The city engineer for a Northwest city knew that the municipality needed a new sewage treatment facility, but his efforts to get the city council to fund it had been frustrating. The council members he had spoken to weren't eager to spend the money, and the new facility was not high on the agenda of any significant block of voters. In that environment, the council members found it easy to ignore the engineer.

Smith and a team of consulting engineers then decided to brief key council members on the project. They prepared a budget and identified potential funding sources. They conducted research into the need for the new facility and into the likely response by different groups of voters. They also clarified the potential consequences of *not* building the new facility, which made a compelling case for addressing the issue now.

If the council members were skeptical of the information provided by the firm that wanted to design the new facility, that skepticism quickly faded when they realized that everything the consulting engineers told them was true. They took the case to the full council and got authorization for the new facility.

Meanwhile, the knowledge of the proposed facility that the consulting engineers developed and the trust they had built with the city engineer and the council ultimately helped the firm win the project.

In this case, an engineering firm built a strong case for a project and convinced the client of the case's validity. The firm's self-interest in the matter was never concealed or in doubt. The buyers (the city engineer and the council members) knew exactly what was going on—and welcomed it. The case that the consulting engineers prepared helped the city officials do their jobs better.

A professional skilled in using a number of techniques is more likely to cross sell business than one who is not, as he will meet more buyers, have more events, and elicit more signals. He will be able to convince a client of the need for his services more compellingly. Most of these techniques come so naturally, many professionals don't recognize them as such!

The techniques most commonly used by professionals are described below. Exhibit 7.1 summarizes them for later review.

Exhibit 7.1
Techniques Checklist

Professionals use techniques to obtain events with clients, identify signals, and advance sales. Review this checklist when you need to do one of these things but are unsure how. It summarizes some of the techniques available to you.

Technique	Description
Asking for Sponsorship	Asking a contact to introduce you to someone else you want to meet, or to advocate for your firm to do a specific assignment.
Pedestal Selling	Talking about colleagues' abilities as if you were putting them on a pedestal to increase the client's desire to meet and work with them.
Presumptive Selling	Acting as if it is presumed that something will happen, such as a meeting with a contact you want to get to know, as a part of a current assignment.
Questioning	Asking clients questions that help them better understand the issues they face and help build their commitment to taking action on those issues.
Seeding Ideas	Stimulating a client's thinking by introducing an idea.
Bridging	Helping a client understand issues that cut across functional or business lines within his or her own organization.
Business Case	Showing why a line of action makes sense from a business perspective, often but not always supported by a simple financial model.
Benchmarking	Showing how a client compares to other firms and showing opportunities for improvement.

Technique	Description
Selling a Vision	Helping a client see a desired future state and how to obtain it.

Asking for Sponsorship

This is the simplest and most direct technique. It is also the one most often mentioned by the people interviewed for this book. Again and again, professionals reported that they simply ask buyers they know to sponsor them. Sponsorship includes asking for introductions to people they want to meet in the client organization, being allowed to attend meetings that could benefit both parties, and asking to be considered for specific kinds of work.

Says Stan Phernambucq, at the time working with URS:

> The same people who bought the original work we did hired us for additional work. They had the need and the money. We wanted the additional work, and they knew we wanted it. You just walk up to them and say we are coming to an end of our work and want to stay with you. They understand, and, if you have done good work and earned their trust, they'll want to keep working with you.

Asking for sponsorship when you aren't used to doing so can seem awkward, but it is seldom a problem for a client who trusts you while understanding your desire for more business. Many of those we interviewed pointed out that their clients want to help them.

Beth Sher, of the law firm Pitney Hardin Kipp & Szuch, learned this lesson when she first approached an in-house attorney, with whom she had worked for several years, for an introduction to his colleagues at a *Fortune* 100 company:

This was uncomfortable for me because I had never thought of myself as a marketer. The man I was approaching is a very private individual. Although he had always been supportive, it was in a subtle fashion. He doesn't praise you much, but he rewards you by coming back to you for more work. If I hadn't known him as well as I did, I wouldn't have been comfortable asking him for help.

The first time I asked him, I raised the subject of our new intellectual property practice. I said that one of my responsibilities as a partner was to introduce other services that the firm offers. I tried being direct but not pushy.

He asked whether I would benefit from introducing other partners from my firm to his colleagues. Because he asked, I told him openly that there was opportunity for intellectual credit and for financial credit. We didn't talk in any detail about this, and he didn't ask for details, but the fact that I would benefit was important to him, because he wanted me to be rewarded if I brought something in. He really wanted to help me succeed, so this discussion helped. He also knew from experience that I would place my client's interests above selling more work.

The introductions this man provided to others in his company were an important step in helping Sher's firm sell additional services.

Clearly, a buyer who trusts you can help arrange meetings for others in your firm, thus benefiting from expertise you may not necessarily possess.

This is what happened when the consulting firm Luminant Worldwide Corporation sought to sell work to a well-known food processing company. The firm assigned a relationship manager to each major account—usually the person with the strongest existing relationship with the client. At first, the firm tried to educate the relationship managers about its other offerings. But this often didn't work, as the offerings were too far-ranging. In addition, a relationship manager skilled at talking with a chief marketing officer might not have the expertise to deal with the chief information officer.

Having learned this lesson, the firm moved to teams of specialists that would work an account together. Jim Corey, who was then Luminant's CEO and president and now heads up Blue Ridge Partners, picks up the story at this point:

> At this client, all we did was build Web sites. We also wanted to help them with e-marketing issues and with procurement. So our creative person, who had been working on Web sites, went to the vice president of e-commerce, her highest level contact. She asked for an introduction to the chief procurement officer, offering to bring in a procurement specialist. This was the first step in our obtaining work in procurement at the client.

When in doubt, ask. Many clients are happy to help you meet others in their companies. After all, if you have done good work in the past, they will want to keep you working there.

Pedestal Selling

Professionals who cross sell services are wise to describe the merits of their colleagues as well, thereby increasing the client's interest in the firm. Many professionals are more comfortable promoting the abilities of others in their firms than they are in promoting their own.

I first heard this called "pedestal selling" by the late Bruce McNaughton, a sales consultant from whom I learned much. He may have invented the term, but it is an old practice. Will Archie, recently retired CEO of the accounting and consulting firm Mitchell & Titus, successfully used pedestal selling with a publishing company. The firm had been working with this client on tax issues.

I invited the new CFO to our offices and introduced him to the client service team: an audit partner, a tax partner, and a consulting partner. I told him that these were the people he should call on if he ever needed help. I was able to say why I had picked each one. As a result of that meeting, we created an opportunity to provide additional services.

A lawyer at a large law firm makes a point of getting to know his colleagues so he can "pedestal sell" those he thinks are superior.

At a meeting with a general counsel, I will say "Hey, I've got somebody in our firm who is really good at 'X.' Do you do any of that kind of work?" They may say "Yes" or they may say "Yes, but we always use 'XYZ firm' for that." In that case, I can always say that if there is ever a conflict, they might use us.

Presumptive Selling

Sometimes it is best to just act as if something is going to happen—and it does! That is "presumptive selling." The client looks to you for guidance on how you are going to conduct your work, and generally accepts what you say about what is needed.

The client expects you to designate whom you will need at fact-finding meetings in order to complete your work. As we noted in the chapter on events, there are three categories of people to consider: those you need to meet with to do your work, those it would make no sense to meet, and those you don't have to meet but who could contribute to the assignment.

You will always meet with the first group and you will never meet with the second group because it would be a misuse of their time to do so. The third group sometimes gets cut out for budgeting or scheduling reasons. But if it would be valuable to know any of these people, put them on the list. The project will be better for it, and you will meet another potential buyer. Of course, if you meet with someone, you must provide value in return for the time you have received.

You can also use presumptive selling to structure a meeting, both to get the job done best for the client and to help you build stronger relationships with people who might buy other services your firm offers. Jeff Boudreau of the consulting firm Kurt Salmon Associates offers his experiences in converting a consumer products client, which had only bought the firm's logistics services into one that bought an array of services.

> When we had key meetings for our logistics project, we made sure that people from different functions attended. They would then be aware of the plans being made, and how those plans might affect their organizations. This also helped us get to know them. Although we had done this to a degree in the past, it was not at such a conscious level.

> We made sure that everyone was actively engaged in the meetings and that we understood their concerns and got their buy-in. We tried to avoid making a presentation, but we did present options and got them involved in the choice. Usually, the team came up with a solution that was a hybrid of several of our options. The participants came to the meeting believing that we were the logistics department's consultants, and left feeling that we were their consultants, too.

This approach resulted in a service the client was highly satisfied with, and it gave Boudreau relationships that he would need to sell other services as the client needed them. Cross selling, when done right, is good for both buyer and seller.

Sometimes it is best to assume that a client will give you an assignment. Steve Vernon, an actuary with Watson Wyatt Worldwide, led a team involved in redesigning a retirement plan for a large electronics firm. While selling his services, he told the client that the administration of the new program would be key to its success and suggested that Watson Wyatt look at that issue, too. The client declined, saying that they wanted to postpone grappling with administrative issues for a few months. Vernon honored that request. But he didn't give up.

> As we worked on the plan redesign, we touched base with the administrators from time to time to keep them abreast of what was being done. In this way, we let them know that we didn't want to design anything that they couldn't live with. We told them about the design we were proposing and asked for their opinions. Mostly they would just nod in agreement, but they appreciated being kept involved.
>
> Throughout this process, we behaved as if we were going to be working with them through the implementation. If a client doesn't like that, they will tell you without being angry about it. Once we started that part of the project, we said, "Here is the budget and the work plan." They massaged it with us and then we went ahead with the work. It would have slowed down the effort and been disruptive to go out to bid. By then they knew we did good work. We could also give them a good price because we were already up to speed on the plan and what they wanted. It made sense for them to keep working with us.

Sometimes things happen just because you say they will happen. If clients know from experience that you will provide value, they will seldom question your plans.

Questioning

People who are good at selling are also good at asking questions. This is as true in cross selling as it is in any other kind of selling. There is so much literature on questioning technique that I can add little to the subject here. Briefly, questions are key to understanding a client's issues and helping the client increase his or her commitment to taking action. "Implication questions," which lead to a discussion of consequences, are fully discussed by Neil Rackham. I recommend his book to anyone who wants more information on the subject.[1] But all good training programs on face-to-face selling teach the use of some form of implication question, though each program may use a different name for them.

Implication questions probe issues such as: What will happen if this problem continues? How much would that cost your company? If this issue were resolved today, how would that help you? Such questions help both the client and you understand the value of a solution to the situation being faced. Those who cross sell well use such questions often.

Hollace Cohen, a bankruptcy attorney at Jenkens & Gilchrist and an effective cross seller, notes that opportunities from other partners are most likely to come to her when they ask the client, "Have you considered what would happen if the company on the other side of the transaction goes bankrupt?"

Once a client thinks about the consequences of such things happening, he is more likely to want to talk with Cohen. Such conversations can result in new business for her, both in providing restructuring advice and in representing the client if the party on the other side of the transaction ends up in bankruptcy.

Asking a question that brings out a predictable dissatisfaction can also be a good way to start a conversation about a service you can provide. Joe Caso, who formerly worked at the accounting firm BDO Seidman, used to ask his clients if they were comfortable with the amount of taxes they were paying.

Also helpful are questions that let you know whether the client knows how to solve a problem she faces. Steve Vernon of Watson Wyatt Worldwide calls these "Whatcha-Gonna-Do-About-It Questions." If the client has doubts about how to deal with an issue, it is a natural lead-in to a discussion about alternatives. That, in turn, makes the client aware of Watson Wyatt's knowledge of the area, which can bring even more business.

Anyone who wants to cross sell successfully should study questioning techniques.

Seeding Ideas

Professionals often "seed" their clients with ideas about subjects related to their services. This can be done overtly and elaborately in a client education meeting, or more subtly in casual conversation, perhaps with a short anecdote about a past project.

You might also bring up an area of your company's expertise because of something you see or hear. Ed Kasparek, an engineer with The Thornton-Tomasetti Group, was visiting a client's offices where his firm was doing a small mechanical engineering project.

> While in the building, I mentioned that we do work on facades and pointed out the window at the overhang. [The client] said they were having problems with water from the overhang, and that he had spent thousands of dollars trying to fix it without success. I said that we had done a lot of work in that area and could bring all our disciplines to bear on it. This was necessary because the problem could arise from one of several sources.
>
> I brought in a specialist and we got the job to do a survey of the issue, which would look at alternative solutions and costs. Then we brought in a group to design and implement a solution. This required both structural and electrical work.

Often seeding is subtle and takes longer. When the head of distribution showed up late to a project review meeting between a management consultant and his company's leadership team, he apologized, saying that he had been held up by a problem in the warehouse. During a break, the consultant asked him about the problem. The consultant then empathized with him, saying he had seen that kind of problem at another firm.

I didn't try to sell him anything because he wasn't ready for it and wouldn't have wanted it. But over the coming weeks when I talked with him, I would ask how the problem was going. After a while he became more comfortable talking with me about the issue and asked about the project I had described in the story I had told. He had remembered it. That led to another assignment.

Ideas can be "seeded" by the way you do your work. Dennis Sullivan, of the consulting firm Robert E. Nolan & Company describes how his firm does that:

Aligning measures and strategy is always difficult. Most companies have broad performance measures but can't tell you how to translate those measures from the boardroom to the mailroom. If we sense that management isn't measuring key items, we integrate those measures into our project. It may cost a little extra, but we see it as an investment. That shows the client the value of the measures and, at the same time, our commitment to addressing their needs.

We can then introduce the idea elsewhere in the firm by talking to, say, the human resources or finance department and asking what metrics they use. Maybe three other areas don't have these measures, so we will tell our contact that we want to use the measures in our presentation to the boss because they could use them in other areas of the organization. You want the client to see that the company needs these measures for its performance measurement to be effective.

Attorney Robert Krauss provides another example of this technique. He points out that due diligence work for mergers or acquisitions provides many opportunities for "seeding."

Say you are doing human resources due diligence and find that there is no process to review past terminations, thus making sure there is no unintentional pattern that could expose the company to a termination claim. You report this to the head of HR at your client, and he says, "Oh, we don't have one of those policies, either." Then you get another assignment.

Many clients expect their professionals to bring them ideas. One consultant told me that the single biggest complaint clients made about his firm was that it didn't bring them enough ideas. Professionals would be considered remiss if they didn't stimulate the client with new concepts.

Once a client sees you as a source of ideas, you are in a far better position to directly cross sell services. Muriel Robinette, of the consulting engineering firm Haley & Aldrich, tells such a story about seeding an idea:

> I had heard through the grapevine that a client of ours had been spending significant money on an environmental problem at one of its plants and that a competitor was in there working on it. I didn't think the competitor's approach was what the client needed, and felt that we had a better mousetrap. But I didn't want to run down the competitor. To avoid that, I approached the issue indirectly.
>
> The director of environmental health and safety at the company liked to keep up on developments in his field. He was used to me calling him about advanced technological issues, so it seemed natural for me to call him on this one. I offered him a free brown-bag lunch to discuss some innovative technologies that I thought would interest him.
>
> I didn't mention the problem I knew they were having, but because I often talked with my contact, I could casually mention our research and development group and its work in the area.
>
> He readily agreed and brought some people together for a meeting, including some from the plant with the problem. I did

enough research to be able to spin presentation to the specific issues they were trying to address.

Finally, they brought up the problem they were having and asked if this approach could solve it. I said it could. That led to a pilot that was so successful, it led to a half-million-dollar job.

The competitor was out—without Robinette having said anything negative about their approach.

Bridging

In the chapter on buyers, I described "bridges" as buyers who worked in many places in an organization and could introduce you to people in many parts of it. Bridges include staff in human resources and information systems. If you are working in different parts of a client's business, you become a bridge for ideas within an account by recognizing various problems or opportunities within an organization that may not seem significant in any one unit. You can also be a bridge by showing clients how to make things work across organizational units. Clients often recognize high value in such help, and it can be an entrée to more work.

DiamondCluster served as a bridge for a client investment banking firm. Mike Palmer tells the story this way:

This client is very "vertically driven." If you are in fixed-income products, you know everything about them but nothing about the equity business or the back office. You get ahead by really understanding one thing, but you don't understand other dimensions of the work, such as how a piece of business will be booked and settled.

We help this company manage across the entire lifecycle of a transaction, instead of simply the act of the transaction. That has allowed us to be introduced in a favorable light into many parts of the organization. They hire very smart people who need a partner who can communicate across the entire lifecycle of a relationship. That's where we provide value.

We offered to teach them how to hire and train people to do this, but they decided that, though they could hire them, they couldn't keep them because the firm rewards being a specialist, rather than a generalist.

Mark Weitzel, of the law firm Thelen Reid & Priest, also sees the value of serving as a bridge and even uses that term for it. He has worked with a large engineering and construction firm and describes the value he provides this client:

I have a joint JD/MBA degree and have worked with this client from the time I joined the firm in 1980. I started working on tax issues for them, and over the last five years, as they entered into joint-venture arrangements, the kind of work I do has evolved. I bring them a series of useful skill sets, including tax knowledge, corporate knowledge, and business sense, which I integrate, providing a bridge function.

Business Cases

Professionals sometimes build "business cases" for the work they are proposing to a client. A business case evaluates the cost, risks, and returns of a specific course of action. This helps the client and the professional think through all the ramifications and value of the proposed work. The story with which this chapter began provides one example of how this technique can be used.

Professionals sometimes talk to a number of people in the client organization and then build a business case by analyzing what hey have learned and offering high-level insights. In such situations, the business case is often the centerpiece of the professional's presentation. Alan Weyl and a team from CSC Consulting spent months at an electronics company on small assignments that allowed them to explore the client's needs. When they had a clear picture, they developed a business case to clarify what they could do for the client:

> We prepared a presentation for our primary contact for [a meeting of the client's top officers from around the world]. It summarized what we had seen and captured the case in what I call "The Million Dollar Slide," which has the whole gig and reason for doing it in one simple slide. It says there is a pot of gold and here is how to get it.

But many business cases are easily worked out in the presence of the client. Again, Mike Palmer:

> If you can't come up with a business case that both you and [the client] believe in, don't do the project. This time we didn't spend much time on it. The value was so obvious, it was done on the back of an envelope. With the kind of payback that we both expected, they had to have that project, regardless of the other issues they were facing. We had people on site who knew the subject matter and had relationships with the controller and others who had to make it happen.

Palmer's firm got the assignment.

The components of a business case depend upon what you plan to do for a client. The case for a cost-reduction project, for example, will weigh the cost of doing the work versus the level of savings expected. The business case for pursuing a litigation strategy is more complex. It must consider the fees and costs associated with the suit, as well as intangibles, such as the impact on goodwill and the publicity it might attract. It must also consider the effect of a course of action on matters the client will face in the future.

Building good business cases for your firm's services is a skill worth having.

Benchmarking

Most clients are eager to hear how they measure up against other companies. Benchmarks measure how a client is doing in a specific area relative to other firms; often, but not always, competitors. They indicate where clients are doing well and where they can improve. Sometimes benchmarks highlight areas where the client needs help.

Tom Murnane of PricewaterhouseCoopers was asked by a CEO with a large entertainment company to facilitate offsite strategy meetings of his management team.

> The entire executive team would attend these meetings, about fourteen people. Once a year it included operations people, too, or about 100 people. I did these meetings two or three times a year.
>
> I charged daily rates for these sessions and spent some time on preparation, which I would bill for. The idea wasn't to make money on this work; it was mostly to help them, but also to better understand their needs so we would provide better service to them. The research was primarily digging up benchmark data, almost exclusively from the public domain. You have to know what you are doing and be sure you are comparing apples to apples. You also have to dissect the data to make sure it is comparable—different companies define things in different ways, for example.
>
> Some of the discussions we had around these benchmarks surfaced issues that later became projects.

Selling a Vision[2]

If a client has a clear vision of a result that he would like to attain, he is usually willing to entertain suggestions about how to get there. That is what selling a vision does for a client, and in so doing, makes it easier for a professional to cross sell services. This technique often requires helping the client redefine a problem it faces. Some professionals are particularly good at getting clients to raise their sights this way.

Henrik Danholt of IBM in Europe used this technique with a large financial institution. The corporation was divided into more than 300 business units spread across the world. This allowed each unit to remain close to its market and be agile, but it fostered a fierce independence. It also worked against capturing the benefits of the company's size, as the business units resisted attempts to get them to share systems or customers. The chairman saw opportunities to increase his company's competitiveness if he could get the unit heads to give up some of their authority and independence for the company's greater good.

IBM developed a concept to allow customers to access services anywhere in the company. It then ran a three-day meeting for every unit head to convince them of the need for it, demonstrating the new system's value to customers. The unit heads were then asked what would happen if a competitor provided that value first. Finally, the presenters showed what the business unit heads would have to give up. In the end, giving customers more value by harnessing the resources of the entire company convinced them to endorse the concept.

Two or more techniques can often be combined. An engineer might combine asking for sponsorship with pedestal selling to introduce a colleague from a different discipline into an account. A management consultant might combine selling a vision with benchmarks or a business case, or both. An accountant might combine bridging with idea seeding. The categories of techniques presented here are not mutually exclusive.

And, of course, there are many other less common ones. But it is time to look at how the four elements of the BEST Selling Model—buyers, events, signals, and techniques—are combined in practice to in-sell services.

8

Summary: Bringing the Parts Together

Professionals who are good at cross selling manage work with these four elements—buyers, events, signals, and techniques—to sell accounts additional services. Review the following story from a strategy consultant and see if you can identify the BEST elements (names have been changed):

I received a call from the head of customer service at a large wireless carrier. Demand for customer service had grown rapidly and unexpectedly, and her department was overwhelmed. We sold her a project to get to the bottom of what was causing the increase in demand and to advise her what to do about it.

I like to sell things that are important to clients. Customer service had one of the largest chunks of human capital in the client organization and was expensive to operate. When a problem has those characteristics, a client will give the resources and information needed to deal with it. A call center is a great front door to what a company is doing throughout the organization.

This was a three-month project. We tracked all the calls that came into customer service for a specific period, analyzed them, and allocated them by issue and cost. By so doing, we developed a database of valuable information for the client. We also interviewed the heads of various business units to get their perspective on the issues, giving us important insights and helping us get to know them.

Early on, I learned that my client's boss, the COO, didn't like consultants. This surfaced when I asked her how others in the organization viewed customer service. When I learned about her boss' attitude, I said, "Susan, if I don't deal with Bill directly, he won't be comfortable with what we recommend and we will be less effective. I don't want you to fight that battle for me." She knew that I wanted her stock to go up in the organization and that if anyone had to take the hits, I wanted it to be me. Susan helped set up a meeting between Bill and me.

When I met with him, I dealt with the issue directly. I told him how we worked and what he would get from our work, and asked him if he was comfortable with that. I also asked if he agreed with our objectives and, if not, how we could reach agreement. This completely cleared the air, and he gave me valuable information about his bad experiences with past consultants. I then asked what kind of interaction he wanted in the future, which gave me direct access to him without going over my primary contact's head. At the end of the conversation, he was comfortable, and so was I.

After that, he became my advocate and started inviting his boss, the CEO, to some of our project meetings. I had suggested to him that the issue we were dealing with was one the CEO had stated that he was interested in, and that it would be good to have him attend a meeting to show his support.

The company was delighted with the results of the project. At each step, we showed them what was happening and how to

reduce costs and improve service. We also helped them understand the market research and brand-management value of customer service. While learning about the client, we determined
how we could build income statements and financials for this
function. The client had never known the true cost of customer
service. Now they did. The CEO could see exactly where the
head of customer service was going to find savings. By the end of
the project, the head of customer service was participating as a
key member of the CEO's management team.

By analyzing all the data we had collected, we could see that
there were other issues that we could help with. Many in the
company had suspected that these problems existed, but now we
had provided the facts.

We presented this information at the end of our final project
meeting with the client. On the last page of our presentation, we
listed four or five important issues and what we recommended to
address them. It was clear that we could help because of the
information we had acquired. It was pretty clear that management wanted our help.

By then, I knew a lot of people in charge of the operations in
question, so I went to them and told them what we had found,
too. By this time, the issues were on senior management's agenda,
so I was giving these people information they needed. I could also
ask what they planned to do about the problems. By then people
were aware of the relationships we had at the senior level.

We worked on only some of these issues because they weren't
all of the same importance. I always want to stay on important
issues and not give the impression that we are "strip-mining" a
client for additional work.

The first additional project we did was to help the company
redesign its channel strategy. Once the vice president in charge of
this area gave the word, we began to analyze their channels.
Ultimately, we helped them save millions in the costs of adding

new customers. Their previous method of adding some customers had brought a deluge of customer service calls.

Next, we were hired by the head of strategy to help rationalize other operations. We were able to use the data from the two previous projects, which helped us do this work for less than we could have if we had started from scratch.

By this time, I was invited to operating meetings and met with the CEO and COO whenever I was in town. They asked us to help design a three-year business strategy. This was quite an honor. . . .

This consultant had never heard of the BEST Selling Model, but she worked with its four elements:

1. *Buyers.* Her story features the head of customer service, the COO, the CEO, the vice president in charge of the channel strategy, the head of strategic planning, and other unspecified department heads. The CEO and COO clearly became sponsors.

2. *Events.* Buyers were met at events, and events were arranged by buyers. These include fact-finding meetings, project review meetings, drop-bys, and a final presentation. The consultant used these events appropriately, not just to complete her initial engagement but also to position the sale of additional work.

3. *Signals.* The consultant received her signals from data collected and from her buyers. She learned that the CEO felt that customer service was an important issue and that problems existed in specific departments and geographic areas.

4. *Techniques.* She applied several of the techniques listed in the previous chapter to obtain events with buyers, elicit signals, and sell more work. These techniques included

asking for sponsorship, presumptive selling, questioning, selling a vision, and building a business case.

This is what real rainmakers, as well as good account teams, do.

The story reveals other aspects of cross selling and in-selling worth noting. First, the process is quite open. Requests for sponsorship were straightforward. Our consultant was not tricking people, but was delivering good service in a way that positioned her to get more work if the client needed it. Clients are business people, too, and they understand and accept this, as long as they feel their interests are the top priority. At any point in the process, if the client had asked her what she was doing, she could have answered with complete honesty. She was doing her best to solve the problem she had been hired to address. She could also have answered, without embarrassment, that her firm would be interested in more work, if there were more services her firm could provide for the client.

Second, this consultant was clearly concerned about her client's best interests. She was only interested in work where her firm could provide clear value; she used information and experience from early projects to save the client money in later ones.

Third, she arrived at a breakthrough point, when suddenly it was easier to sell additional work. This often happens during cross selling. A professional does well on one assignment and maybe two, then suddenly finds it easier to sell multiple projects.

This is because the professional has gained so much insight into the client's needs and people, it is easier to recognize more opportunities and get to the people who must deal with them.

In addition, a "tipping point"[1] is reached when the professional becomes familiar to so many people in the client organization, he or she is immediately considered the problem-solver in specific situations. The professional's comfortable relationship with the client's senior management also works in the consultant's favor.

The formalization of the BEST Selling Model allows us to manage this process deliberately. At regular internal meetings, where a firm discusses a specific project or account, the account manager can ask the following questions of the team members:

What events, with which buyers, did each of you have since we last met? A good account manager will want to monitor the team's events, not just to complete the current assignment but to position for additional work.

What signals did you obtain at these events, if any? By asking this question at each account meeting, the manager trains team members to look for signals. Once a signal has been identified, it should be tracked to see if other sources can validate it. Developing back-up for its importance is the next step.

Which additional buyers, if any, did you identify whom we want to get to know? The account team needs to identify the buyers for other services the firm offers, especially when a signal indicates that there may be a need for a service. By asking this question at every meeting, the account manager increases the team members' awareness of the need to identify buyers of additional services, while completing their current assignment.

Which buyers do we want to meet with next? It will be easier to sell additional work if team members have developed relationships with relevant buyers. If this can be done in the context of the current work, the professional firm gains a huge advantage over competitors.

What events can help us meet them? Events are key to managing cross selling because they can be scheduled. By monitoring the events held with each targeted buyer, the account manager can monitor the progress of the team as it seeks to develop the account. A quick review of the menu of events in Chapter 5 allows team members to identity events they can use to meet with the targeted buyers.

What techniques do we want to use with which buyers to achieve these events? Similarly, team members can review the list of techniques provided in Chapter 7 to identify techniques to achieve the required result. Do they want to ask for sponsorship? Do they want to presume that it will be arranged because it is necessary to complete the current assignment? Or do they want to use some other technique?

What are the objectives of the event? In addition to gaining information required to complete the current assignment, what objectives does the professional have for the event? Is it simply to begin or advance a relationship with the buyer? Is it to validate and learn more about a signal heard elsewhere? Or is it to increase the client's commitment to taking action on an issue? The objective you set will determine how you handle the meeting.

What techniques do we want to use at those events to elicit more signals or to increase the client's desire to give us more work? With the objective in mind, the account team members can review the list of techniques shown in Chapter 7 to select those that will best enable them to achieve it.

Implementing the BEST Selling Model requires asking these questions at each team meeting. Asking these questions alone is not enough, however. Other things must be in place to allow your people to cross sell effectively. The second half of this book deals with those issues.

Part II

BEST Selling Within the Context of the Firm

Part I of this book shows how professionals cross sell, describing what they do in terms of the BEST Selling Model. Part II describes two things:

1. What you as an individual professional can do to make yourself a successful cross seller; that is, to make the model work for you.
2. What firm management can do to institutionalize cross selling by putting the model to work within an organization.

As individual professionals and managers, we have a limited number of levers we can pull to enhance cross selling.

The first of these is the allocation of resources. Firm management can select account managers and assign them to accounts. It can also assign other professionals and staff members to the accounts, can free up time for account development, provide a budget, and provide an array of other marketing resources. The individual professional can also allocate his or her own time to cross selling, whether or not firm management asks for it.

The second lever is communications. Firm management communicates through policies and procedures, through the requests it makes of people, through organized communications programs, and through systems that aid information exchange. Individual professionals communicate with their words and actions. Each kind of communication can be used to support the cross-selling effort.

Finally, there is the rewards system. This is largely a prerogative of management through bonuses, raises, and promotions. But the individual professional can also self-reward if his or her efforts aren't being recognized by others. Most of the remaining chapters deal with aspects of these levers.

9

Allocating Resources to Accounts

Cross-selling strategy is implemented through the allocation of resources, specifically talent, time, and money. If we want to cross sell, we must allocate sufficient resources to account development. This is true for both the individual professional and for management in large and small firms.

Even when acting as an individual professional, you can develop accounts on your own initiative. When the sales of one consultant tripled in only a year, I called him to discuss what had happened. This is what he told me:

Almost all of my additional sales came from the two clients I was working with a year ago. When I compare these accounts to the ones I had worked on earlier in my career, the difference is obvious. While at the old clients, there were maybe two or three people I would feel comfortable calling, today with the current accounts there are twenty or thirty, working in many parts of the organizations, whom I could call. I have gone out of my way to know everyone I could. The head of information technology at one of the companies even refers to me as "the account manager." This is strictly because of the way I behave because I have never been given that title. In my old accounts, I didn't even know the head of IT because that isn't a function that my practice normally deals with. Because I know so many people in the accounts and understand their issues, I am able to sell them an array of services.

Thanks to his success at cross selling, the consultant was promoted to partner and later formally appointed as the account manager for these clients. As often happens in the professions, the title was given as recognition that he was already performing as a partner and account manager, rather than in anticipation of what he would do in the future.

The description of the BEST Selling Model in Part I of this book tells you how you can develop accounts. But you have to devote the time. As we have seen, much of this time can be leveraged time (i.e., time you would spend at the account in the course of completing an assignment).

Management's allocation of resources to account development has several major components: assigning account managers, selecting account team members, setting budgets for account development, and providing a variety of kinds of staff support.

Account Management

Get the right person to do the job and the job is already half done. In fact, selecting the right account manager is probably the single most important thing management can do to ensure that services are cross sold to a major account. As a partner at one Big Five firm once said:

The best successes we have had with long-term relationships came from the efforts of one or two service leaders in an account. These sellers are always bringing opportunities to others, bringing in project after project. They are able to leverage their relationships back to their colleagues in other parts of the business.

Here are some of the traits you'll want in an account manager:

A Person with Strong Relationships at the Account

A person chosen to manage an account will have a leg up if he or she already has strong relationships there. Picking such a person can save you time and money.

But it may happen that no one at your firm has strong relationships at the account. Even more troublesome, the person who does have relationships may not possess the other attributes of a good account manager. When such a person is chosen for the job, at best the account doesn't get developed. At worst, you lose it. Let me repeat a story told in the introduction to this book because it is so relevant:

> Susan, a laterally hired partner at a large professional firm, was assigned to an account team. The client bought only one of the firm's many services, and the firm expected her to introduce others. She quickly learned that the partner in charge of the account didn't want her help. Although he had been chosen for his presumed strong relationship with buyers in the account, he always had an excuse about why he couldn't introduce her to anyone there.
>
> When she researched the company, she realized that she knew a senior person there and called him. It had been intended as a low-key conversation just to catch up, but after they had talked for a while, her contact began to complain about the way her firm was providing services to his company.
>
> Susan said, "He said that we were making decisions they should be involved in. They felt that the partner in charge of the work acted as if he were smarter than they were and always knew

best. They wanted more teamwork and more services, but they weren't comfortable talking to him about their needs."

Susan almost got killed because she was new to the firm and it appeared she was just trying to take an account away from someone else.

But the client was adamant about having the current account manager replaced. He was. Within a year, the professional firm had increased its sales to the client five-fold and was selling them an array of services there worth many millions of dollars.

As this example shows, the temptation to assign the job of account manager to the person with the strongest relationships at a client should be resisted, if that person doesn't possess other required qualities. The firm was missing the chance to cross sell. Worse, it might have lost the client if the account manager hadn't been replaced.

A Person Who Wants the Job

Someone who is motivated to do the job will, of course, be more likely to succeed than someone who is drafted.

A Person Skilled at Building Relationships

The account manager must be willing to build relationships with many people throughout the client organization at varying levels. To develop relationships with senior management, the account manager needs both interpersonal skills and the ability to understand and discuss the client's business issues. We will address this subject in more detail later.

A Team Player

Only team players succeed at account management. The job requires working with people from other practices to cross sell their services. "Lone Rangers" don't do this well.

A Person Well Connected Within Your Firm

Having knowledge of the services your firm offers and the trust and good will of others in the firm will help a professional introduce other services to the client.

A Person Who Is Long-Term Oriented

Account managers must want to work within an account year after year. To succeed, the client's interests must always come first. This means that doing the current assignment well is the first priority, good relationships are second, and selling additional work is third. We will further develop this subject later in the book.

Unfortunately, most firms have few people who meet all of these criteria, so they must select those who meet many, and help them develop in the areas where they fall short.

It is usually best if an account manager manages a small number of accounts. Many work only one large account, some two, and a few three. I know of several firms where management realizes that assigning more than a few accounts to a manager is counterproductive, but they do it anyway. When that happens, the account manager either focuses attention on one or two accounts, almost ignoring the others, or focuses on a few relationships in each account where sales are easy. Neither approach is likely to produce the desired results. It is best to focus on fewer accounts, making the hard choices required to do so, or else hire and develop more account managers.

The Account Team

The makeup of the account team depends upon the range of services your firm offers and the size and complexity of the target account. Team members usually include:

- Professionals who are currently working in the account and have established relationships there.

- Representatives of practices not currently working in the account but who would like to. These representatives often have expertise in the account's industry.
- Other people in the firm with relationships to key buyers in the account, such as those who worked for the client company prior to joining your firm.
- An assistant account manager, often an account manager in training, to help the account manager with administration.

Though the core team should be relatively stable, its membership need not be fixed. For example, someone completing a short, one-off project for a client may participate for only a few months.

When teams become larger than seven or eight people, they may become unwieldy. However, the complexity of some accounts requires many people on the team. In such cases, the account manager may bring the full team together only a couple of times a year. At other times, he or she will meet with the core team, and then separately with subgroups, such as the North American or European members of the team.

Even with careful selection, some team members will prove unproductive. Some excellent professionals simply don't want to participate in this kind of teamwork. Unusually heavy workloads or family problems may prevent others from participating. Those who consistently fail to cooperate with the team's efforts by missing meetings and failing to follow through on commitments will drag down the performance and morale of the team. Every firm that sets up account teams should provide account managers with the ability to purge nonproductive team members.

Management can also help the account teams do their jobs better by providing simple staff functions like distributing recent articles about the account to more complex support, such as analyses of a client's business issues and a mapping of these issues against the firm's available services. Several firms have done this by developing solution sets.

Solution Sets

Solutions sets[1] are arrays of services provided by different practices that can be bundled together in different ways to solve a specific, complex problem, say the selection and installation of a large software package. Because many clients are likely to have the problem that solution sets solve, firms can train people on how to market these services together and provide a variety of support to the sales effort, such as proposal boilerplate. A law firm might develop a solution set of services to help a client deal with an acquisition, for example.

Developing solution sets can help your people evolve from a linear view of cross selling to the sale of integrated solutions.

Firms wishing to cross sell for the first time often begin with a fantasy of passing a client seamlessly from service to service as the client and the firm work through the solution to a business problem together. It is seen to be like a relay race with one practice picking up where the other leaves off. In reality, management will quickly stumble over a number of obstacles, making the seamless approach hard to execute.

First, professionals are protective of their client relationships, and rightly so. A good professional makes it clear to a client that at all times the client's interests come first. He feels awkward going to a client as his practice nears the completion of a piece of work to offer additional services from someone else in the firm. It makes him feel like a salesman. The less he knows about another practice, the more likely this is to be true. In addition, he doesn't want to hand his client off to someone else.

With the seamless model, there is also a giver–taker imbalance between the practices that works against a relationship of mutual support. The professional who works with the client first is placed in the role of the giver to whom others must come begging for help, hat in hand. The beggar can quickly become surly if repeated requests for access to the client are rebuffed. This is when you hear absurd accusations like, "You control the client. You ought to be able to get me in."

If a handoff is made this way, it is seldom seamless, especially if the giver and the receiver are working together for the first time. There are typically overlaps and gaps between the practices' services. If these aren't recognized and dealt with quickly, confusion can ensue when the second practice begins its work. At best, that can be embarrassing.

The solution to this problem is much the same for the professionals in your firm as it is for the client. As we have discussed in earlier chapters, clients have an easier time buying several services from you if they see from the beginning how those services fit together to solve a complex business problem. Selling such a vision is the essence of selling an integrated solution. It may be a vision of a move from a regulated to a deregulated environment, or a vision of the successful acquisition and integration of another firm or some other vision. But it is always the vision of a total solution.

Typically, a professional presents the vision to the client early, before work begins, or during the portal project. That way the client knows from the beginning that an array of services will be needed to solve the problem. From the very beginning, then, the professional discusses with the client all the things to be done to solve the problem. Client and professional discuss which of these are best done by the client's own people, the professional firm, or third parties. The professional is doing little selling—rather, he is designing a solution with the client. After the client buys the overall vision of a solution, individual services will be brought to bear as they are needed.

Selling a vision works for your own people, too. If people from several practices see how their individual contributions fit into an integrated solution, cooperation becomes easier. It is easier for the first person working with the client to introduce a comprehensive solution to the client's problem. No longer is one person giving entrée to a client for others in his firm. Instead, a team works together to solve a single problem. All stay involved in appropriate degrees, and service gaps and overlaps between practices tend to be dealt with early in the work design.

The preceding paragraph makes it sound easier than it is, but selling a vision of an integrated solution *is* often much more effective than the seamless approach.

Of course, someone has to sell the vision. Doing so is easiest when the lead in the sale is taken by an experienced cross seller, a professional with a broad knowledge of business issues who understands the array of services your firm offers and who has a flare for solution design. But that person isn't always in the right place at the right time. Perhaps no one in your firm has much experience cross selling. For people with little cross-selling experience, it's hard to sell a vision of a solution to a complex problem.

The task is made easier if a firm has assembled solutions sets. Again, a solution set is a set of services that can be assembled in a variety of ways to address a specific kind of problem. That problem might be a client's need to enter a new market or to divest an operation, or achieve another complex objective. The professional then draws on services from the solution set to address the issue. This process can be compared to a modified job shop in the manufacturing sphere.

A modified job shop lies between a pure assembly line operation, where every final product comes out the same, and a custom shop, where each final product and the components that comprise it are unique. The best example we have seen was a plant that manufactured industrial sewing machines. The plant's customers needed different machines for different purposes, including sewing buttonholes, cuffs, or inseams. The different purposes required machines with different characteristics. For example, some required more power than others, and some handled material one way and some another. Machines for different purposes were designed to be built from a limited number of standard parts. There were, say, three kinds of motor, five kinds of housing, two kinds of spindle, and so on.

Each kind of machine also had a limited number of unique parts. For example, the foot, where the material is moved under the needle, tended to be specially designed for each kind of machine, depending on its specific purpose. The reliance on a limited number of parts made both design and assembly easier than if each kind of machine had been totally unique.

The same is true of solution sets. By educating your people on how the different services your firm offers can be assembled to address a specific kind of problem, you make it easier for your people to design an integrated solution and sell it to a client. Exhibit 9.1 shows a hypothetical example of solution sets.

Exhibit 9.1
Sample Solution Set

	Buyers			
	Title A	Title B	Title C	Title D
Issue #1	Service 1, 2, 3	Service 1, 2	Service 3	Service 3, 4, 5
Issue #2	Service 1, 2, 6, 7	Service 1, 2, 6, 7	No Service	Service 3, 5
Issue #3	Service 1, 2	Service 1,2	Service 3, 8	Service 3, 4, 8, 9

Across the top of the matrix are the job titles of the people the different practices at the firm in question are most likely to sell to.

Down the left side are listed some of the major business issues that clients are likely to ask the firm to address. The cells of the matrix are populated with the services that might help people with each job title solve each kind of problem. The entries in the cells are the piece parts from which an integrated solution can be assembled. They are like the different kinds of motor and housing for the sewing machines. Each assembled service is different, but it is built largely from standard components. Once a professional becomes familiar with the parts at her disposal, and with the people who deliver them, it becomes much easier for her to assemble an integrated solution.

Knowing this, firm management can educate their professionals on how their different services can be used together. They can bring together the people who deliver the different services, so that they can work out how to mesh the services and become familiar with each other.

When poorly executed, the sales of solution sets becomes nothing more than a series of product sales pushed at the client. When done well, it makes it possible to sell an integrated solution to many buyers within the client organization. The sewing machine salesman may stress the durability of a machine's motor to the customer's maintenance staff while focusing on the special design of the foot to the quality control staff, all the while selling the whole machine. So, too, the professionals at a firm can stress those aspects of their services most relevant to each person they talk to. For the professional inexperienced at selling integrated solutions, the availability of a solution set can make the job easier.

Solution sets are no panacea but they can help jump-start a cross-selling effort at firms with limited experience. They have been highly effective with several firms that have grown by acquiring smaller specialty firms because they can speed up the integration of the new services.

Solution sets are developed through the following steps:

1. *Identification of issues and champions.* The firm must decide what issues to develop solution sets around and who is going to champion their development. Most firms select issues by reviewing recent exciting projects and selecting from among them those that seem to deal with hot but complicated issues. They look for a professional who, based on a successful recent project, would be an enthusiastic champion for developing the solution set.

2. *Selection of task forces.* Next, the firm must assign a task force to each solution set. It will comprise people from relevant practices with experience dealing with the issue in question. Each task force must then develop a schedule and budget to create and circulate material necessary to promote the solution set within the firm.

3. *Materials development.* Each task force must develop an issue statement, explaining why the issue is key to clients and the value of a solution. That statement must be supported by:

   - *Case studies.* Concise examples of cases where the firm has helped clients deal with the issue in question. If possible, there should be examples of several different ways to assemble the services that make up the solution set to meet different client needs.

   - *Service descriptions.* Short explanations of the services the firm offers to deal with the issue and who at the client would be most interested in them.

   - *Sample proposals.* Boilerplates that can be modified to address new opportunities to provide the solution set.

   - *Presentation slides.* Slides that can be modified and used when presenting the solution set to clients.

   - *Contact information.* A list of contacts the professionals in the firm can call for more information about each service included in the solution set.

- *Staff education.* The task force must then educate firm partners on the solution set. This can be done at large firm meetings, at presentations to account teams, or in one-on-one meetings between task force members and other partners.
- *Promotion.* Task force members can promote the solution sets by writing articles and giving talks on the issue in question.

As we have seen, properly developed solution sets can be a powerful cross-selling tool.

If you are going to assign your staff the responsibility for cross selling, you will want to be sure that they are equipped to do the job. One resource increasingly given to account teams requires special attention. Many accounting and consulting firms are beginning to add business developers and dedicated salespeople to their staffs. Architecture and engineering firms have already successfully worked with such people. Getting your salespeople and your professionals to work together is a special challenge that deserves a chapter of its own.

10

Professionals and Salespeople: Mix Well Before Serving

With John Mirro

Increasingly, professionals must team with salespeople to bring in work at major accounts. While ten years ago this teaming was confined to architectural and engineering firms, today it is common practice at accounting and management consulting firms, too. Only at law firms are dedicated salespeople still a rarity. (If you are a lawyer or at a consulting firm that chooses not to use salespeople, this chapter may be less useful for you.) The mixing of salespeople with professionals is happening for many reasons and in many ways, as the following examples show:

- A computer manufacturer and service provider found that many of the buying decisions for its products were being heavily influenced by consultants. At the same time, declining margins for hardware made it increasingly difficult to provide services at the low fees the company had traditionally charged. To deal with both of these issues, the firm developed its own consulting arm. The arm, made up of newly hired consultants and former members of its services organization, was expected to work closely with the company's massive sales organization.

- A small performance-improvement consulting firm designed a sophisticated, multistage sales process built around an executive-level sales force. The business that this sales system generated helped the firm grow rapidly into a major force in the consulting industry.

- A software vendor added systems integration services to increase the attractiveness of its offerings. Over time, the service offerings broadened and deepened while the sales of software products declined. Eventually, the firm eliminated its software products, so completing its transformation to a consulting firm. The sales force, which had initially sold only software, now sold only services.

- A publicly held technology-consulting firm needed to maintain its rapid growth rate to meet the expectations of the financial community. Its consultants were so stretched by the needs of its existing clients that they weren't developing new ones. It added a sales force to fill this void.

Most of the organizations that have tried to get consultants and salespeople to work together have found the problem difficult. There have been notable failures:

- A hardware manufacturer and technology service provider built a consulting organization at huge expense by recruiting consultants from many well-known firms. The consultants and salespeople clashed. Efforts to get the two organizations to go to market together were undercut by turf wars. These were based on the conflicting beliefs that the head of the consulting arm and the head of the sales department held about the roles of their organizations. Many of the consultants left the organization, both voluntarily and otherwise, after about two years.

- Impressed by the success of a competing performance-improvement consulting firm, another firm hired away some of its salespeople and tried to duplicate the other's success. The salespeople proved far less effective in this new environment. They were unhappy with their role in the new organization, and the consulting staff largely saw them as unproductive overhead.

- Another firm added a sales force to help it grow rapidly. After a year of large expenses and few sales, the sales force was let go.

- A large accounting and consulting firm hired a sales force to increase its growth rate. It found that the newly hired salespeople were highly effective in some regions but not in others.

High Stakes and Mutual Arrogance

Getting professionals and salespeople to work together is, then, a high-risk venture. The payoff can be huge, but the potential for an expensive failure is also great. Success comes, in part, from understanding the different attributes of these two kinds of people and designing an approach that works for both. Failure often follows an effort to glue a sales force onto a professional firm or a consulting team onto a product company without adequate preparation.

Salespeople and professionals have fundamentally different orientations. There are many kinds of professionals and salespeople, but the two groups have general tendencies shown in Exhibit 10.1.

Together, the attributes shown for a good salesperson make up a persona who is quite different from the typical professional. A good salesperson is motivated, trained, and compensated to sell. He or she takes great pride in this ability, sometimes to a fault, and aggressively promotes both self and product. The sale is the pinnacle experience; everything that follows is a necessary detail. Peak performance is demonstrated by making the quota club year after year. Some salespeople arrogantly believe that they can sell anything.

Exhibit 10.1
Tendencies of Salespeople and Professionals

	Salespeople	Professionals
Motivation	Make the sale	Solve the problem
Compensation	Commission	Billability
Strengths	Sales skills, Relationships	Technical knowledge Analytical ability
Source of Pressure	Quotas	Schedules & budgets
Source of Pride	Finding opportunity, closing sale	Objectivity, professional skill
Ultimate Achievement	Making quota club	Making partner
Purpose of Team	Get the sale	To complete the work
Potential Arrogence	"I can sell anything."	"Only a professional can sell our service."

Salespeople typically do not follow procedures well. Sales is a process, and a professional salesperson will adhere to his or her own successful process. But the organization that tries to hold a salesperson to an institutional procedure risks losing its salespeople.

A good professional is motivated, trained, and compensated to solve the client's problem, using technical ability and professional knowledge that takes years to develop. Naturally, the professional takes great pride in these skills as well as in objective reporting, which clients value. Completing a successful engagement is the pinnacle experience; everything that precedes that is simply a means to an end.

The ultimate achievement is being made partner, a position that certifies success with clients. Some professionals arrogantly believe that no one but a professional can sell professional services. In some areas of the professions, such as systems integration consulting and architectural project management, good professionals will follow procedures carefully because they understand that success in project delivery is one built on uniform procedures and methodologies.

While we believe these generalizations reflect actual tendencies of those who are salespeople and professionals, the differences are so vague it can be hard to get people to see them. Professionals, for example, will often say that they, too, are motivated to sell. This is true, but generally not to the same degree as with salespeople.

Most sales teams at one time or another, get caught way behind on their numbers near the end of a quarter. At times like this, the team must pull out all the stops to bring in its committed revenue. Every path that might lead to more revenue is explored, no matter how difficult or uncomfortable that path may be.

Executives who have signing authority are called at odd hours just to increase the chance that they will, instead of their administrators, pick up the phone. Sales representatives may wait in lobbies or in parking lots trying to get one more opportunity to ask for the business. These tactics push a client's patience, but the experienced business developer can do these things because he or she has built such a strong relationship with the client.

Professionals who are closely aligned with the sales team wonder how so much revenue can be generated in such a short period of time.

When all is explained by the successful sales representative, the professionals find it difficult to ever picture themselves in that situation and find it difficult to believe anyone could accomplish such things.

True Sales Grit

Can you imagine a professional in this situation? At the end of a quarter, a sales team at a software developer and consulting firm had achieved only 10 percent of its assigned sales goal. One representative on the team was working on a transaction that, if closed, would put the whole team over the top, but this transaction was complex and involved contacting and obtaining agreement from numerous executives at several distant customer locations. The sales representative went to the office of a key executive and brought the other buyers together via conference call. He pushed to have this transaction completed by midnight. This was a highly uncomfortable situation for everyone. But it gets even worse.

As the negotiations continued, it was clear that there were some significant legal hurdles to overcome. The sales representative had to keep every client executive on the phone with his own company's legal staff until just before midnight, when all the legal issues were resolved and the transaction was signed.

Most professionals couldn't and shouldn't behave this way. It would be inappropriate in their role as professionals.

Many professionals will say that they, too, have strong sales skills. However, in our experience, more claim them than have them. Their professional knowledge and client experiences carry them, reducing the need for sales skills while blinding them to their own shortcomings in this area.

A consultant from a leading technology company recently told us that, in his opinion, most consultants have just enough sales knowledge to be dangerous. He illustrated his point with a story about a consultant who consistently tried to sell a new project to the group where he was engaged. He knew the requirements cold and couldn't understand why he consistently got "no's" from his contacts. He then related his experiences to the sales team, telling them that, in his opinion, the sale didn't have a chance.

Fortunately, the sales team knew that none of the consultant's contacts had the authority to say "yes," and that the authority lay several levels up in the organization. The sales team worked at the proper level and eventually sold the project. Working at a level where the decision-maker has the authority to say "yes" is a basic sales skill, but it might be one which is not always taught to professionals.

Of course, salespeople often fail to appreciate the strengths that professionals can bring to a sale. Not long ago, a salesperson estimated a fee for a job to develop a small application. He based his estimate on an experience he had had with another client the month before. The two jobs looked exactly alike to the salesperson, and he based his proposal on this knowledge. When the consulting team reviewed the proposal, they determined that the project should have been priced for twice the amount of hours. An embarrassed sales representative had to resubmit his proposal to an upset prospect because of a small technical detail with profound implications that had escaped his notice. Had the salesperson involved the consultants early in the sale, the problem would have been avoided. This example shows why few words strike so much terror into a professional as when a salesperson says, "I just sold a project for you."

What You Can Do

Given these differences between professionals and salespeople, it is no wonder that getting them to work together successfully can be challenging. Here are some things you can do to increase the chances for success.

Make Sure That You Want a Sales Force

As the examples listed earlier reveal, a sales force can add substantial value to some professional organizations but not to all.

Some practices do not lend themselves to using dedicated sales forces, and some firms are unwilling to make the basic changes required to allow a sales force to succeed. This is not a change to be taken on lightly, nor is it an essential change at all firms; some highly successful firms do not use dedicated sales forces.

Make Sure the Commitment of Cooperation by Senior Management Is Clear and Visible

The success of any change effort requires the support of senior management. Those who run the professional and sales organizations must be selected for their interest in cooperating and must demonstrate their commitment to it repeatedly. Differences in opinion about how the two groups should cooperate should not be based in turf wars at this level. It is hard to imagine how a program to get professionals and salespeople to work together will succeed without commitment to cooperation at the top. A number of attempts have foundered for the lack of it.

Design the Organization for Cooperation

Managing large accounts is a complex job, especially if the firm sells work to several of the client's business units and is providing services from several practices. Every bit of information gathered about the client is critical, not only to ensure current client satisfaction but also to construct plans for future sales. When the professional team and the account management team work in a spirit of cooperation, information will flow freely and all parties will benefit, including the client. The account management team will be more attuned to the challenges facing the client and will therefore suggest solutions to real problems, as opposed to simply presenting their latest offering.

To foster success and growth, management must construct an organization in which the flow of information between the sales and delivery organizations is not only encouraged but required. First, this is an issue of organization design. There is no one right way to design a firm so that professionals and salespeople communicate, but the need for this communication must be central to any design.

Second, a firm can establish procedures to bolster communication. Several simple steps can be taken to start the information moving between the groups. These include encouraging regular meetings between the salespeople and the professionals working an account. Reports on the status of client work can be shared with the sales team. If you don't feel that the sales team can be trusted with this information, something is wrong with the way the salespeople are selected, trained, and managed. All employees of the firm should be expected to respect client and project confidentiality. If this standard is rigorously enforced, communications within the firm can be more open. Informal gatherings, such as social events, are also a good way to help professionals and salespeople get to know and trust one another.

Recruit Salespeople and Professionals Who Are Predisposed to Cooperate with each Other

Most selling of large projects will require teams. There is little room in this environment for "Lone Rangers" who want to sell on their own. The most successful teaming of professionals and salespeople has occurred where the team members want to work with each other and appreciate each other's strengths. One large accounting firm that added a sales force was successful, in part, because the salespeople it recruited were enthusiastic listeners when working with the professionals.

Establish a Career Path That Allows Professionals to Become Salespeople and, if They Have the Right Credentials, for Salespeople to Become Professionals

If a sales force and a professional staff come from entirely different backgrounds, the probability of a "them-versus-us" mentality will greatly increase. The best professionals, of course, can sell effectively, and the best salespeople have good analytical minds. A little effort will permit you to develop career paths that allow people to move back and forth between roles.

Alas, that is seldom done. In one large firm, we were told that sales positions had been offered to consultants but that none of the consultants wanted to become salespeople. For that reason all of the salespeople were being recruited from outside the firm.

We asked what this was costing and learned that recruiting fees were running the typical 30 percent of first year's compensation per hire. Given the number of salespeople being recruited, this added up to a large sum. At the same time, the firm was spending nothing at all to make the sales positions attractive to consultants. After that, development programs were put in place to help consultants become salespeople.

It can be difficult for a professional to make the transition directly from doing professional work to entering sales. Providing a path with intermediate steps often works better. One software firm we know has brought consultants into the position of pre-sales system consultants. This gives them the opportunity to work directly with the customer and the sales team before the sale occurs. Once they have done this job, they are more likely to succeed at pure sales jobs.

Create Opportunities for Salespeople and Professionals to Work Together

Professionals who hold key account knowledge should always be made part of the account sales team. They should participate in regular staff meetings. Care must be taken to respect their time since they are billable, but the loss of an hour of billable time spent with the account management team is insignificant when compared to the benefits obtained.

Professionals in lead positions should be invited to participate in selling classes at which workgroups map out sales. These practice sessions give the professionals a clearer idea of what is and isn't important to a sales team when formulating a strategy to support the client's needs. It will make them better listeners for sales opportunities when they are on site with clients.

Similarly, salespeople should attend key project planning meetings and major client meetings. Professionals sometimes fear that, if invited, salespeople will not act properly. However, they can only learn by experience. Their added knowledge of the client, and the professionals' contribution, will enhance their future effectiveness, both with the account and with the professionals.

Establish Compensation Systems That Encourage Shared Goals and Cooperation

People are driven by their firm's compensation plan. A sales representative will listen to firm goals and objectives but will act in his or her own best interest—and that interest is to maximize income. It is essential to create a compensation plan that rewards the salesperson for cooperating with the professional team, and vice versa. We will address compensation issues further in Chapter 13.

Well-planned efforts to get professionals and salespeople to work together can reap huge rewards. The investment in adding a sales force to a professional firm or a consulting arm to a product company is so large, this planning will ensure that you will get your money's worth.

11

Rules of Engagement

To cross sell, people from different parts of your firm must work together. The larger and more complex the organization, the greater the need for ground rules followed by everybody involved. Establishing those rules is a job for management. These ground rules must be few, simple, and make sense, or your people will ignore them. They must make it clear that the clients' interests are paramount. And they must be focused as much on liberating your people to cross sell as on placing one or two needed controls on the process.

If you are not a member of management and management fails to provide any rules, you should establish your own that you can follow consistently and articulate to others. Once you have worked with a colleague from your firm and been on several sales calls together, the rules become less important. But until then, they can help avoid confusion.

Here are some rules that we have found work well. If some of them aren't right for your firm, then you should clearly articulate alternatives. The first four rules are about the importance of the client's interests.

Clients' Interests Come First

A hallmark of professionalism is putting our clients' interests ahead of our own. Every cross-selling decision should be consistent with this rule, and management should reinforce this rule visibly and often. If you need to decide whether or not to take a representative of another practice to a client meeting, ask yourself if doing so will add or subtract value for the client. If it will lessen value, the other person shouldn't go.

It is fair to ask someone who wants to attend a meeting what value he or she will add. That value need not be added at the meeting in question. For example, having the account manager at a meeting may assist the top people in the client's organization, because the account manager will come away with a broader or deeper understanding of the issues the client is facing. He or she can later build upon that understanding to add value at other meetings.

But if there is a real risk that the newcomer will reduce value to a client, that person shouldn't be introduced. Rainmakers, open to introducing people into their accounts, are adamant about this. A partner at a Big Five accounting firm who is extremely effective at cross selling goes out of his way to meet people and learn about their services so he can offer more to his clients. But first these people must pass the value test. He tells this story:

> You have to know and trust the people you are introducing to your client. I had a guy [in the firm] who told me he wanted to talk [with a client] about merger and acquisition work. I said to come on down and tell me what you've done. He kept telling me about what the firm had done, but not what he himself had done. I finally said, "But what the ____ have *you* done?"

The partner later decided not to make this introduction.

Of course, this rule can be abused. Some professionals refuse access to an account to everyone at their firms. They may feel that if they introduce someone else and the client is unhappy with that person's work, the client's interests will not be well served. But this is really just risk aversion.

There is always a risk of something going wrong with any service a client buys from you. If you feel a specific service that your firm offers is weak, then don't make the introduction. But if you believe that you are the only one in your firm who can provide value to a client, then you are at the wrong firm.

If we deny someone else access to an account, we must always question our motives for doing so. Are we concerned about our client's interests, or are we really concerned about our own security or the political power we derive from being the sole contact at an important client? Introducing someone else sometimes does mean that we must sacrifice something for ourselves. But if it is in the client's interests, we should do it without hesitation.

Putting the client's interests first sometimes means foregoing revenue. Notes Stephen Quinn of HNTB:

> I've passed on jobs I could have won because I didn't have the right people to do them. To take them would hurt my reputation. Clients understand, if you explain it to them.

Sometimes putting the client's interests first means giving revenue to other parts of the firm that you could keep for your own practice. David Keyko, of the law firm Pillsbury Winthrop, notes:

> A client may want an alternative dispute resolution (ADR) clause in a major contract. The firm could either have a corporate lawyer draft this part of the contract or bring in someone from the litigation department. The corporate attorneys can do a perfectly good job, but the litigators do bring expertise when the client is contemplating how to structure the resolution of potential disputes.

Involving litigators in drafting the ADR clause also gives them a chance to establish a relationship with the client. If they aren't introduced at the drafting stage, there may not be a chance for the client to get to know them before a dispute arises. Then it may be too late and the client may select another firm whose litigators it already knows. Also, if they have drafted the ADR provision, the litigators will be familiar with it and better able to help the client.

In the end, putting clients' interests first comes down to a mindset. Says Connie O'Hare of Mercer Management Consulting, "My philosophy is about serving clients. In the process you do sell things, but that derives from serving clients. It is different from a philosophy where your first priority is to sell clients something."

Whenever there is a disagreement within your firm about how or what to sell next at an account, revisit this rule.

No One Controls the Client

Clients control themselves and it is, at best, presumptuous to suggest otherwise. We *serve* our clients by providing professional *services*. Most professionals know this, but the rule needs stating for those few who are confused. If, on occasion, a professional at your firm claims to "control" an account, he or she is dangerous to the firm's ability to maintain the client. The expression reeks of arrogance. Arrogant people can sometimes win business, but they often lose accounts.

Sometimes professionals will claim to control an account in order to protect the client from disjointed approaches by many different practices. Their claim becomes more strident if someone else in the firm has approached the client in an inappropriate way. But they should not be given control. Rather, the firm needs a clearer process for managing the client relationship.

At other times, a professional is said to control a client by a colleague who wants an introduction. The speaker usually says, "Because *you* control the client, *you* ought to be able to get *me* an introduction." This is wrong-headed. Ultimately, clients decide who they will see and who they won't. Others in your firm may be able to influence their desires, but they do not control them. When someone in the firm says that she cannot or should not introduce you now, there is a good chance she is right.

We Must Never Be, or Seem to Be, More Interested in Selling the Next Assignment Than in Doing the Current One Well

We are being paid to deliver a top-quality service, not to sell more work. Getting the work done well that we were hired to do must be the top priority of everyone associated with the engagement. To place getting the next matter ahead of succeeding with the current one violates the rule of putting the client's interests first. Clients are sophisticated and quick to recognize a sales effort.

If I see that you put my interests ahead of your own, I will allow you to sell to me. But if I sense that you just want my money, I will resist.

The Account Manager Represents the Client's Interests Within the Firm

Of course, everyone working in an account must represent the client's interests. But in a large account, where a firm provides a number of services to different parts of the organization, someone must be responsible for the client's interests at a level higher than that of a specific piece of work. A service that one practice provides to one part of a client has implications that go beyond the issues that practice deals with. A problem the client has with one practice affects other people at the firm. The account manager must deal with the account at that higher level.

It is because the account manager has this responsibility that she should be invited, if at all possible, to any meeting she wants to attend. The person in the firm responsible for the meeting may be the one who makes the final decision, but he should bend over backwards to accommodate the account manager.

The account manager also needs to have the ultimate say about pricing and other issues that would normally be the domain of the practices. Take this example: A consulting practice at a Big Five firm was working at a company that had stopped paying its bills. The partner in charge of the project complained to the account manager that the client owed about $1 million. Says the account manager, an auditor:

> I called [the client] and he said he was unhappy with the work and was sitting on the bills on purpose. He wasn't going to pay anything. I listened to his concerns and told him that I would revise the bills and come back with a new number that I thought was fair. I did that and went back and he said that was fine, that that was what he had wanted. He paid.
>
> The real issue was that he had a number that he didn't want to exceed each month. If we wanted to work in this account, projects had to be done in pieces that would be within this constraint. That was how he worked. I knew that, and the consulting guys had known that, but either they had forgotten or they had gotten authorization lower in the organization and so felt they could ignore it. As long as this guy was our primary sponsor in the account, we had to accommodate him. I had to get the consulting guys to change the way they worked to do that.

If the consulting practice's relationship had been the only one at stake, the problem might have been handled differently and by different people.

The next set of rules is about ownership.

The Individual Owns the Relationship, but Not Exclusively

Relationships are between people, not between companies. If I have a relationship with someone, it is personal and inseparable from me. It is based on time we have spent together, experiences we have shared, and mutual help. I can no more give it to someone else than I can give away the relationship I have with a friend.

And no one else can take it from me. Someone else from my firm might have a relationship with the same person, but that will not threaten mine, as long as I continue to provide value. Their relationship may be stronger or weaker than mine. It will certainly be different. We can both talk to this client and have good conversations. Those conversations will differ because our relationships differ.

Multiple relationships, then, are good for the client, as long as value is received from all of them. That a client gets calls from several people from your firm is also good for the firm. It shows that the firm has bench strength and cares about the client. A client not only can but should have a relationship with more than one person from a firm.

Of course, all parties must coordinate communications so they don't trip over each other by calling the same person on the same day for the same reason. But that is an execution issue, not a rule of ownership.

The Firm, Not an Individual, Owns the Account

The individual owns the relationship, but the firm owns the account. Contracts are made with the firm, and the client's checks are made out to it. The firm has the legal obligation to pay salaries and rent, and it gets the money it needs to do these things from the accounts. It therefore has a legitimate interest in them.

Also, the firm has paid your salary while you pursued an account. You used the stature and resources of the firm to sell and deliver work there. Without the firm, it is doubtful that you could have won or maintained the business.

The firm's ownership of the account gives those who run the firm the right to ask you how well you are managing it. They also have a right to ask you to introduce other services when it is appropriate to do so.

The Account Manager Represents the Ownership of the Firm

In firms that assign account managers, the account manager represents the interests of the firm. Anyone in this job is charged with looking after the client's interests first, the firm's interests second, and his own third.

Often the account manager is simply the person with the strongest relationships at the account. As we have seen, that person may put personal interests above those of the firm. For reasons explained in detail in the introduction to this book, it is usually in the interests of the firm to sell multiple services to an account and to serve the client in several locations and in several business units. It is good business to do these things *as long as they are in the client's interests, too.* Anyone who cannot distinguish between the client's interests, the firm's interests, and his own should not be an account manager.

An Introduction to an Account Must Be Earned

Just being a partner or an employee of a firm doesn't give you the right to be introduced into any of its accounts. You have to earn that right. You must invest time getting to know who in your firm is working the account, help them understand what you do, and explain how you can provide value. In these education sessions, never over-sell what you can do.

You should also invest time learning about the client and its needs. Because your firm is working at the account, the client naturally expects you to know something about its business.

If someone from the firm introduces you into an account, you must put the client's interests first, the firm's second, and yours third. This means that if a colleague at the firm introduces you into an account because she knows you can help solve a problem the client has, you help solve the problem. You do this even if the problem is smaller than those you would normally deal with. You do so because you don't want to disappoint the client, the firm, or your colleague. Afterwards, you may want to give your colleague some guidance on how to better screen opportunities for you, but you won't leave him or the client in the lurch. If you do, don't expect to be invited in again.

Because the person who introduces you to a client puts her reputation and a valuable relationship on the line for you by doing so, she is likely to retain a legitimate interest in the quality of the work you do. It is only fair that you accept that interest and keep her informed of how things are going. This is especially true if anything goes wrong. Says Bruce Tindale of PA Consulting, "The person making an introduction often chooses to remain closely involved in the ensuing sale and client work. This allows him or her to transfer knowledge about the client and to act as an informal quality control assurer."

Of course, if you have the relationship at the account, you have a responsibility to give others in the firm a chance to earn your trust, and with it help get access to the client. This means spending time learning about other people in the firm and what they do. It means making yourself available to them when they want to talk about what they think they might be able to do for your client.

The newly assigned account manager at one big firm tried repeatedly to meet with a partner who had an important relationship at the account. The account manager had years of experience working in the client's industry and had a good relationship with several people at the client company. Still, the partner made it clear that he didn't want to help the account manager advance his relationship. He failed to return the account manager's phone calls and canceled meetings repeatedly. Finally, he promised the account manager an hour of his time. When they met, the partner opened the meeting by saying, "I've only got two minutes for you." This man was not fulfilling his responsibility to give a colleague a chance to earn his trust.

An Individual Owns Every Event

Someone in your firm must own every meeting with a client. It should usually be the person who, in the client's eyes, has primary responsibility for it. That person decides who gets to attend the meeting and what the agenda is. She should be open to suggestions from others, but she decides who gets to go and what will be talked about. Unless this rule is followed, you risk confusing the client with competing agendas.

Participants at an Event
Must Follow the Agenda

This rule is particularly important when members of a firm haven't worked with each other in the past. It helps ensure that the client doesn't feel misused by having a meeting originally designed to get work done unexpectedly turn into a sales meeting. To avoid embarrassment and frustration, the professionals and the client must have clear and shared objectives for each meeting. Without such a rule, they very likely will not.

A newly hired member of the consulting arm of a large telecommunications company once took a salesperson to a meeting with a former client, the CEO of a large bank. The consultant saw it as an opportunity to briefly describe his new position and to hear about the client's network communications needs. When the CEO mentioned the bank's plans to change some of its telecommunications infrastructure, the salesperson piped in with,

"We would like a chance to help with that." The CEO gave the consultant a withering look. Neither the CEO nor the consultant had seen the visit as a sales meeting. The CEO was not the appropriate person to sell equipment to. When the salesperson had seized the chance to push a sale, the CEO felt tricked, and the consultant later had to call to apologize.

Everyone from your firm who attends a client meeting must follow the agenda. Only the client has the right to change it.

There are also two rules about communications.

Everyone Working for an Account Has an Obligation to Keep Others Informed

To service an account well requires good communication among the people from your firm working there. They need to tell each other about macro- and micro-signals that they hear from the client. They need to let each other know about events they have scheduled, especially if more than one person from the firm is likely to schedule an event with the same person at the client. They need to give each other information that will help all people from the firm do better work for the account.

A well-run account program will have an established communications system. This subject will be addressed in more detail in the next chapter. But regardless of the level of sophistication of the system in place, each person working in an account has the obligation to keep others in the firm informed about things they need to know about an account. It is in both the client's and the firm's interest that each person does so.

No One Has to Ask Permission to Call Someone He or She Has a Relationship With

This is the most controversial of the rules and one that may not fit every situation. However, I believe it is fitting most of the time. If

I have a relationship with someone in an account, I own that relationship. I have the responsibility to maintain and develop it and I cannot do those things unless I talk with my contact from time to time. I should not have to ask permission to do so.

This right to call people I know does not relieve me of exercising good judgment. I should not call my friend if someone else in the firm is waiting to hear whether the client has hired her for a large piece of work because the client may misconstrue my reason for calling. I must also keep other people informed about what I am doing. But I don't need permission to call.

In firms where people must get permission to call, contacts tend to shrink over time to only those between the account manager and his contacts in the account. Some account managers might be happy with such an arrangement, but it isn't healthy for the client or the firm.

These rules should help people organize themselves around the cross-selling effort, but they alone are not enough to get the job done. The next chapter discusses how to overcome the functional thinking that can be such an obstacle to cross selling.

12

Overcoming Functional Thinking: Cross Selling and Communications

With Dallas Kersey

The managing partner of the New York office of a medium-sized consulting firm was caught by surprise when his team learned that one of their cornerstone clients had decided not to give them a major new assignment. They had worked hard to win it, but the client contact told them he had chosen someone else whose bid was lower. Who won the business? The consulting firm's Washington office. No one in the New York office had had a clue that another of their offices was bidding against them.

This is fact, not fiction, an example of geographic cross selling out of control. Could it occur again? "I really don't think so," comments the managing partner. Are there new rules, tighter controls, new monitoring procedures to avoid that problem? Firms often resort to such dire measures when problems like this one arise. But he gave none of these reasons.

Instead, the managing partner believes it won't happen again because of improved communications. Forget the carefully worded e-mail messages, internal newsletters, and rules and regulations. They have a place in successful cross selling, but only a limited one. A more effective, though often underutilized, mechanism to both promote cross selling and help your people avoid tripping over each other is an effective nurturing of communications. The pitfall is to think of communications too narrowly ("A couple of meetings should do the trick") or too casually ("Let's send out an e-mail to solve this").

Effective cross selling requires communication about two things. First, the professionals must know the client and understand the client's issues: What are the political sensitivities, what services is the firm currently providing the client, and who has key relationships there? Second, the professional must know all about the firm that employs him or her. What services does it offer, what are the signals that a client might need these services, who are the key contacts in each practice who can help sell them, and who can you trust to do a good job for the client?

Both the individual professional and firm management must take responsibility to acquire and share this knowledge.

The Individual Professional

Communications, in the context of cross selling, can build mutual trust and professional respect. Without these two ingredients, no effort or initiative from the firm's leadership will convince an individual professional to allow another into the client sanctuary.

"You have to have the utmost confidence in another partner," comments Pat Pollino, vice president of marketing and communications at Mercer Management Consulting. "The toughest sell is your own partner."

Mutual trust-building starts with you; do not wait for someone else to reach out first. Although trust is an obvious need between professional and client, many find it more difficult to accomplish within their own firm. Creating trust is fundamental to effective cross selling, and you must devote time to building it.

In addition to trust, cross selling requires professional respect. No one in his right mind is going to jeopardize a relationship with a client by introducing professional mediocrity into the mix.

Anita Porter (name changed) was the account manager and audit partner for a global company. Fees from the company were about $65 million annually. She had already introduced a number of partners into the account, so she was clearly willing to cross sell services. But she didn't respond when a tax partner in her firm asked to meet her client's CFO. She did her homework first and decided that there was not enough professional respect to introduce him; he had just been relieved of his role with another client because of risky tax advice.

If you don't earn the professional respect of your colleagues and learn professional respect for them, nothing that management does will increase cross selling. Below are some things you, as an individual professional, can do to build the communications base you need to cross sell.

Network Internally

External networking is essential for successful selling, but internal networking may be even more critical—for survival. Be curious, ask about another professional's field of expertise, find out what his or her clients' needs are so you can spot a similar need at your client. This would seem obvious and easy to accomplish, but in practice it isn't. The standard reason: Everybody is too busy.

Change that standard. Try to have one meeting a month with a representative of another practice to learn about those services and your colleague's professionalism. Exhibit 12.1 provides a list of questions you can ask.

Exhibit 12.1

Cross Selling Interview Questions

Here are some questions you can ask a colleague from another practice to be better able to cross sell his or her services.

- *How do you describe your practice?*
  Even if you know what other practices do, let people you interview describe their services in their own words. They will usually be different from the words you would choose, and for good reason.

- *What kinds of companies do you sell to? List some representative clients and the work you did for them.*
  Let them describe their markets in their own words. Descriptions of past work will give you examples to use when pedestal-selling your colleagues to a client.

- *Whom do you sell to in the client organization?*
  This will help you identify people that you know who might want to meet your colleagues.

- *What are some common signals that a client might need your services? What are some of the hot issues you are dealing with now?*
  Answers to these questions will help you identify opportunities for your colleague.

- *What are a few questions I can ask that will help me screen opportunities for you? How big does an assignment have to be to interest you?*
  You only want to introduce a client and a colleague if the meeting would be valuable for both of them, so you want to be able to screen out opportunities that only seem attractive on the surface.

- *Whom do you compete with and how do you differentiate yourself from these competitors? If a competitor is already serving my client,*

what might be good reasons for introducing you?
The chances are that your client is already working with a competitor of your colleague, and you will need to be able to explain why he or she should meet with your colleague anyway.

• *How can I help you?*
Maybe the colleague knows what help he or she wants.

———————

Add the colleagues you meet this way to your contact list, so that you call them periodically to catch up, learn the latest information on what they are doing, and remind them of your interest in sharing leads. Take one idea a month to your client, using a colleague as the expert in the subject. If you start introducing others, they will begin to introduce you. This is a win-win situation: The client wins, and both you and your partner win.

People who cross sell are eager to know about what their colleagues do, and word gets around that they are receptive listeners. Bob Hirth, a partner at Andersen, is such a person. His enthusiasm for learning about services his colleagues offer can be heard in his voice. He tells this story:

> I am the [account manager for a large technology company in the process of making layoffs]. One of our tax guys came to me and told me about some ways to reduce payroll tax exposure during layoffs. I can now talk about this with [the technology client] and with other clients. You get this kind of information formally and informally, but the idea is to be broadly aware of other services and intensely interested in your clients' needs, so you can make the right matches.

As this story suggests, such meetings with colleagues can help educate you about the kinds of business issues that your client is likely to face. That can help you hold a relevant, if brief, conversation with your clients on a range of topics outside your specialty. Truly knowing the people you will be introducing to your client will help you do so with confidence. That confidence can be essential, as this story by an attorney shows:

> The best business is when you can get more from an existing client. I have a client, a manufacturer with maybe two dozen plants in the United States. It was founded by two guys I have been close to for a long time who are chairman and vice-chairman. Because of that relationship I get the favor of the first shot at any legal issue they've got.
>
> Recently they had a major labor problem: The Teamsters were trying to organize one of their plants. I knew the plant manager, too, and suggested he use us, but he had used someone else in the past who had done a good job for them and was considering using him on this matter. I knew our labor attorneys and could say with confidence that our firm has a top-notch labor practice, so I decided to push for a shot at the work.
>
> The plant manager knows of my relationship with the chairman and said that if it was okay with the chairman, it was okay with him. I called the chairman and he said, "If you want it, I trust you. All I want is to win. I really don't care what lawyer does the work as long as we win."
>
> This was really hard marketing. I had to go to the plant and do a lot of things, but our guys won the case and we got $400,000 out of it. I could have taken the position that if we lost the case and the Teamsters got in, I would end up on an ice floe as far as the client was concerned. But you have to take the risk.

That risk is easy to take if you have confidence in your colleagues because you have taken the time to get to know them and learn about their specialties and their character. Of course, the same thing applies to you in reverse. If you take the time to get to know others, at the same time, they get to know you. That will make it easier for them to recommend you to their clients.

Exhibit 12.2 provides some indicators that should encourage your trust and also some that should give you caution.

Exhibit 12.2
Trust Signs

Here are some signs that a colleague is to be trusted to cross sell effectively with you and some signs that suggest caution. Of course, you will be judged by the same signs.

Good Signs	Bad Signs
Willing to spend time to learn about your services.	Only interested in telling you his or her own services.
Offers help even if only in small ways.	Often asks for help but never offers any.
Willing to introduce you to a client.	Always has an excuse for not introducing you.
Fulfills promises.	Often makes promises that he or she doesn't keep.
Is honest and open about problems with clients. Knows that everyone has had them.	Never admits to having any problems with clients.
Is open and honest about strengths and weaknesses of his or her service. Knows that all services have them.	Never admits to any limitations of his or her service. Seems ready to take on any assignment without hesitation.
Can cite specific past work to illustrate points about his or her work.	Always talks generically.

Good Signs	Bad Signs
Will stand by you to help you and your client, even at some cost to himself or herself.	Walks away from any assignment that doesn't fit his or her established profitability profile.
Finds time to help you even when busy.	Always too busy to help.

Know the Client

Some professionals think that because they are specialists, they can only provide value to the client in their area of special knowledge. Yet, their work at the client often gives them a unique perspective on the client's issues that the client finds valuable. A litigation support consultant may be able to abstract from the work she is doing for the client to help the client avoid litigation. An engineer may be able to see things about the way a client manages its facilities that is costing money unnecessarily. An executive recruiter may learn things about the way a client integrates newly hired executives into its business that help the client retain them. Professionals who bother to look beyond the immediate task they have been hired to complete can often see things about a client's organization that the client doesn't.

"As we peer into a company, we have a new perspective and lens through which to see their issues. It's a great advantage to be able to see what others can't or don't see themselves," says William Shine of Kepner-Tregoe, a consulting firm.

But this requires a genuine curiosity and asking many questions. This curiosity should not be restricted to one's expertise but should focus on the client's business. Questions to ask both the client and oneself include:

Why is the current assignment important to the client? How does it relate to major initiatives the client is working on? Don't assume you know the answer to this question; ask. You will be surprised at what you sometimes learn. The information you gain will help you do a better job for the client and allow you to observe more insightfully.

An industrial designer recently asked this question of a client for whom he was designing electronic equipment. The client responded, "I used to be in charge of the business unit responsible for [product A] and built it up until we had a 25 percent market share. In my new job I am responsible for both [product A and product B. For Product B] we have only a 2 percent market share. That is unacceptable."

This information gave the designer a much better insight into the client's business and personal needs than he had had before. The urgency of the project was far more obvious than when he viewed it as simply one to help the client increase market share.

What patterns do you see from the work you do, especially patterns that are apparent across several assignments? What gaps do you see in the way the client is approaching its major initiatives? Patterns and gaps can provide insight into things the client could do better, and they can provide signals for additional work. They may simply provide extra value to your client from your current work. Clients often value such observations when they are introduced tactfully.

Carol Benjamin of William M. Mercer was working with a client that was rapidly growing from a regional to a global company. It was now hiring many people from outside the company; previously, it had promoted from within. Management was also being forced to think globally for the first time. Benjamin noticed that the company was not managing these changes as effectively as it might. When she shared this with the client, she was pleased to receive a positive response. In fact, the client welcomed the chance to talk to an expert on change management from her firm. The ensuing discussion provided high value to the client and led to more work for Carol's firm.

Professionals sometimes don't ask these questions because they are unsure of the response they will receive. But how would you feel about a doctor who noticed a potentially important pattern related to your health but didn't bother to ask you about it because it wasn't his specialty? In contrast, how would you feel about a babysitter who asked about any difficulties your child was having at school, so as to be better able to help the child during the evening? When asked as an appropriate sign of concern, questions that go beyond the immediate work are usually welcomed by clients.

Providing value in this way is easier if you understand something about business drivers, the fundamental factors that determine a business's success. We frequently hear management at firms complain that their people don't understand their clients' business issues. That makes it difficult for them to talk to people in the client organization who work in areas outside their specialty. Management often says that this weakness results from a lack of understanding of fundamental accounting, but, while a knowledge of accounting helps. We have heard the management at accounting firms complain that many young accountants don't understand business issues, either. Reading the business and trade press and the client's annual report and Web site will help gain this understanding. So will reading business literature.[1]

Adopt the Role of Cross Seller

Often professionals are reluctant to approach new prospects in their client's organization, either because they feel uninformed about the services of their own firm or uninformed about the client.

I once attended a meeting at which the new partners of a firm were told of their responsibilities as partners. Among them was the responsibility to cross sell. All of the partners admitted that they didn't know enough about the firm's other services to try to cross sell. They felt that they would need to know almost as much about the firm's other services as they did about their own.

This belief alone showed that they were victims of functional thinking. Like many professionals, they believed that they had to be an expert to sell a service to a client. To cross sell, professionals must escape this mindset, although it is hard due to the way most professional careers develop.

Early in their careers, most professionals have faced a client who was reluctant to use them because of their youth and inexperience. Young professionals overcome such skepticism by demonstrating functional expertise—showing that they know a lot about a topic such as environmental litigation or marketing channel management. When clients recognize this expertise, they tend to accept them in spite of their youth. The image of the skeptical client, however, lingers on, even as the professional grows older and more experienced.

As professionals build expertise, their functional knowledge becomes a primary reason to involve them in sales. A seasoned rainmaker will probably manage the sale, but the young expert gets to attend the meeting, reinforcing the message that functional expertise is essential to selling. It is little wonder that many professionals see that if they lack expertise in the full range of a firm's services, it can be an obstacle to cross selling later in their careers.

Cross selling does require *some* knowledge of the other services your firm offers, but not as much as you might believe. This is because selling and cross selling are different jobs, with different responsibilities. A client expects different things from you when she asks you about services she expects you to provide and when she asks about the services that she knows other people in your firm will deliver. You need to know and do different things in these two contexts.

Within your area of specialty, the client expects you to understand the technical details of her issues. She expects you to design a service that will meet her needs and to oversee and participate in its delivery. You are responsible, then, for scoping the assignment, pricing it, closing the sale, and delivering the work either directly or through your team.

When a client comes to you with a problem *outside* your area of expertise, she expects something else. She knows that you don't know enough to fully scope the problem and design a solution by yourself, and may well lose confidence in you if you try. She is turning to you because you know her and her company, and so, she believes, you will understand the broad context of the issue that she is addressing.

She also looks to you to find the right people in your firm to solve her problem, both in terms of their technical ability and their potential match with her people. This allows her to save time and money on searching for a professional, and increases her chances of getting the right people for the job.

She comes to you because she trusts your judgment and your professionalism in placing her interests first. Once you have introduced other people from your firm, she expects you to help mediate the work design and the sale based on your knowledge of how her firm works. In addition, she expects you to serve as guarantor of service quality and an advocate for her within your firm if things go wrong.

This role as cross seller is made clear in this quote from Jeff Boudreau, a management consultant at Kurt Salmon Associates. Boudreau, who specializes in logistics, had been working at a direct-to-consumer company for several years.

Last week I got a call from the CIO [whom I had met on other projects] asking us to come in and propose an information technology strategy project. He was looking to me as a conduit to the firm to put together the right team because I knew the company so well. He knew that I could assemble the best team, and that it would be difficult to bring someone else up to speed. Even though my work has been in logistics, he wanted me to guide the team. Some of their fulfillment issues are very complicated, and I understand them. That means I can provide insight for the information technology project.

Overcoming functional thinking, then, requires moving from the role of seller to one of cross seller, with all that implies.

Keep Others Informed

If you are working with a large account, go out of your way to inform others from your firm about what you are doing and what you are learning. Look for systems in your firm that will make this easy. If there are none, or getting new ones is slow and bureaucratic, invent your own—phone, e-mail, whatever. But do share information.

Your firm can reap the benefits of multiple relationships only if those working in an account share what they learn. If there is no formal system for sharing information, assume that responsibility for initiating the process starts with you. All good leaders recognize the value of good communication.

One of the world's largest systems consulting firms, which installs customer relationship management (CRM) software systems, didn't have its own CRM system. The management of one big account was suffering because those working with the global client, some forty-five people, had no efficient way to keep each other informed of what they were doing, their contacts in the account, or the import of recent meetings. The partners managing the account solved the problem by buying an inexpensive commercial software package and borrowing some space on a server to house the application. It was a jerrybuilt solution compared to the ones the firm developed for its clients, but it provided the means for those working on the account to keep each other informed. These partners recognized how critical good communication could be.

Keeping communication flowing within your firm (both regarding clients and what you are doing for them) also builds something else: trust. Open communication breeds a sense of trust in others.

Lean on the Institution That Is Supporting You

You are not serving your clients alone (if you are, you shouldn't be). There are lots of smart people in your firm who possess a great deal of knowledge and expertise that could be brought to address your client's issues.

Management at one firm was concerned that its professionals were being distracted by too many e-mails each day. To identify the source of the problem, they commissioned a study of e-mail content. This study showed that 80 percent or more of the e-mails asked questions such as "Do you know so-and-so in this company?" and "My client needs help in this area. Who knows anything about the subject?"

Certainly, a good argument could be made that the firm needs a more sophisticated way of handling this information, but that's not the point. These professionals network continually, leaning on their institution to better serve their clients.

Institutional Communications

Firm management must use communications as a tool to increase cross selling. It must clearly communicate the importance of cross selling and how it expects the firm's professionals to make it happen. It must provide venues for representatives of different practices to share information on their services, on their clients, ,and on cross-selling opportunities.

Leaders of professional services firms that are effective at cross selling do the following:

Set the Pace

Leaders who are out cross selling set the pace. The definition of "leader" shouldn't be a handful of the most senior people in the firm, but should include practice leaders, office managers, industry leaders, or the like. For cross selling to work in large firms, leaders at all levels must set the example. They must foster a culture of "Do as I say and do as I *do*."

Minimize the Rules

The most frequent concern that our clients express about increased cross selling is the risk of clumsy and overlapping contacts to the same people in the client company. There is a tendency to avoid this problem by setting strict rules governing client access, but rules won't get the job done, especially if they create hurdles your professionals must overcome before they contact a client. Rules requiring clearance from an account manager before a call is made into the account can only create frustration and slow down progress.

These rules are often less necessary than they might seem. We once attended a meeting of some thirty senior partners of a firm who were trying to revitalize its marketing effort. The managing partner was encouraging all the partners to contact former clients. To avoid having several people contact the same clients at the same time, several partners quickly moved the discussion to the need to coordinate the effort. When the managing partner suggested a simple solution based on people exercising good judgment, several of his colleagues adamantly opposed, saying the approach was too risky. When the partners were asked if anyone could remember a client ever saying that he had received calls on the same day from two people in the firm, only one person raised his hand.

This man had been the most vocal advocate of elaborate contact rules. Some months earlier, he had been meeting with a client executive when the client left the room to take a call. On his return, the executive informed the partner that the call had been from someone else in the partner's firm, trying to set up a marketing visit. The partner was furious.

"But what was the client's reaction? Was he upset?" the other partners asked. "No," admitted the partner, "he thought it was funny." No harm had been done, and the partners decided to go ahead with the system based on exercising sound judgment.

Also ineffectual are rules that insist the professionals introduce representatives of other practices to their clients. Professionals resist attempts to force them to introduce others. Note again that the rules outlined in Chapter 11 are few, and are as likely to be about freedom of action as about limitations. Few professionals in our experience will first turn to the firm's rules regarding cross selling, but they will refer to them as a backup if a conflict arises.

The managing partner of a large accounting firm once called the national partner responsible for marketing and asked, "What are the rules dealing with cross selling?" Surprised, the marketing partner responded, "I'm not quite sure. Why do you ask?" The answer (we hope in jest): "Well, if I don't know the rules, I can't break them!"

You will want to create enthusiasm around cross selling with a strong focus on understanding and fulfilling clients' needs. If you have that, there is need for only a few cross-selling rules.

Get People Together

The most successful cross selling occurs when professionals who know and trust each other work together to solve a client's problem. Even with today's communications technology, people are most likely to cross sell a service if they know it will be delivered by a colleague they trust.

Communication and cooperation are actually affected by the layout of your offices. Studies have shown that as distance increases in feet, the frequency of informal communication declines rapidly.[2] Some firms have rearranged offices to increase communication among those who need to cross sell each others' services.

Many firms that cross sell well provide opportunities for their people to get together, learn about other practices, and build trust. Whitney Pidot, an attorney at Shearman & Sterling, introduced the firm's intellectual property practice to one of his clients. His ability to do so was enhanced by efforts made by the head of that practice, who had begun to educate others in the firm about his services. Says Pidot:

> The head of the practice has made presentations at our practice committee meetings. This group meets monthly and consists of the heads of practices and the worldwide offices. He has also gone on the road with a number of his people to visit our offices and make presentations there.

The firm encourages this kind of behavior.

Another law firm, McCarter & English, has a different structure for the sharing of information about practices. As attorney David Osterman describes it:

> We have seventeen practice groups in our firm. Once a month we come together and pair up a couple of people from each group, and then we exchange information on each others' practices. This month the product liability group may sit with the tax, estate, and trust group. Next month, they will sit with someone else. We talk about the work we are doing, and we tend to know each others' biggest clients. But the best cross-selling opportunity may not be at the biggest client. The smaller client may have a greater need.

A firm can set aside a central fund for leadership to bring people from different backgrounds together to investigate a common issue.

Maybe it's a client or prospect, an industry segment, or an emerging trend that could be addressed best by professionals from several practices. They have not yet had the opportunity to build trust with each other, and welcome such invitations by management.

If you want your people to cross sell, you must bring them together to build their knowledge and trust. This is true in bad times as well as good. One professional put it bluntly:

> The dumbest thing is not to hold a retreat when you are short on cash. You make back the money you spend on the retreat as soon as your people hit town because of the cross selling. You need to get your people together. That's where cross selling occurs.

Celebrate Success

Successes at cross selling should be celebrated to show that the cross sale is valued and to publicly recognize those responsible for it in a way the monetary rewards don't. Celebrating shows clearly that management wants more of this kind of effort.

Each firm needs to calibrate these celebrations according to its culture. Here are three examples:

- One firm recognizes cross-selling efforts at its quarterly partner meeting. Each success is described, and the partners stand and applaud.
- Another firm's culture permits more bravado: For a day after a cross-selling success, everyone in the office wears a whistle and blows it randomly to celebrate.
- A third firm has a wine-and-cheese party for everyone in the office on the Friday evening after the success.

Recognize Best Practices

There is a high probability that your firm already has many examples of cross-selling successes. Less happily, you will also sometimes learn of the cross-selling successes of competitors.

Management can encourage cross selling by making sure that fundamental lessons from these examples are shared across the firm. Unless management takes the initiative, the sharing of the stories is likely to get stalled by the imperfect communication that exist in all organizations and the egos of those who are uncomfortable recognizing that a peer or competitor may be doing better in some area than they are.

When asked to help coach account teams at a large firm, we suggested that each team meeting start with a story of a success achieved by another team. Each success-of-the-month story would have a simple structure. It would describe what had been done and the result, and give the clear message that this was what management wanted, if it could be duplicated by others. The management team collectively scratched their heads over this suggestion. Finally one senior officer said, "Well, that certainly would be counter cultural." At this firm, professionals felt uncomfortable talking about anyone's successes but their own.

If you can't share successes, each account team is doomed to reinvent solutions to cross-selling problems again and again. Management must make sure that that doesn't happen.

Provide Tools for Sharing Information

Professionals need tools—simple or complex, inexpensive or expensive—to facilitate information-sharing that is essential to cross selling. The bigger and more complex the firm is, the greater the need for these tools.

But many professionals are reluctant to share information about their clients. Entering information into a system can also be seen as a time-consuming nuisance.

"I like this new system and can't wait to use it," commented the Taiwan office manager of a global consulting firm. But he went on to add: "Certainly no one in this office is going to spend any time entering information in the system for others—unless they pay us to do it."

One senior executive, Robert McKee, Watson Wyatt Worldwide's head of marketing, has dealt with this issue and had this to say:

> A global firm serving global clients is compelled to have global marketing and customer relationship management. We cannot serve our clients well if we are not formally sharing client information among ourselves. When we serve a client in, say, seven or eight countries, we have to have the systems in place working for our people so that they can communicate better. There is no "well-maybe-but" alternative. This always raises large cultural issues, which have to be addressed and worked through.

A firm needs three kinds of systems to support cross selling:

Client Contact Information

Systems providing this information are increasing in sophistication and are now commonly now called customer relationship management (CRM) systems. The term CRM, in professional services firms, has become synonymous with big and expensive. Perhaps this is because of what we hear about large, multimillion-dollar and multiyear CRM installations for large companies. But there are other approaches that can be scaled down to meet the needs of professional firms of all sizes.

First, you must get consensus within your firm about the precise information needed to better manage business development and cross selling. At a minimum, you need a record of the contacts your professionals have in client and prospect organizations. This should include each contact's name, title, company, address, phone number, and e-mail address. This sounds simple, but it isn't based on stories from sophisticated firms.

"Oh, you mean mailing lists," offered one senior professional. "We have lots of those around here. In fact everyone has his own. We find it almost impossible and expensive to go through the process of trying to invite clients and prospects to a seminar. It takes months to get a list together!"

Firms are at a disadvantage from multiple lists developed for different purposes. Some of these lists are thorough and some scanty. Some have one set of information and some another. All are dated. There are many kinds of commercially available systems to help you consolidate this crucial information, ranging from simple, standalone packages to integral parts of more sophisticated CRM offerings.

Whatever your firm's view of contact management systems, one thing is obvious: Those contacts are a major asset.

A Record of Your Business Pipeline

Managing the business pipeline in a professional firm is an art. Certainly each professional knows what's in his or her own pipeline. But even in firms as small as twenty-five people the important information about opportunities being pursued is often either not known, tracked informally through discussions, or out-of-date and incomplete. "We tell our clients they can't run their businesses this way, yet we do it to ourselves," observed a business development consultant.

Information on the business pipeline will help firm leadership recognize opportunities for cross selling that may have been overlooked by the professional leading the pursuit. A good system allows you to identify such opportunities early, when it is still possible to influence the structure of the solution being suggested to the client.

Account Intelligence

For the whole of your efforts to be more than the sum of the parts, account team members must share what they know about the client. This includes information on major developments at the client, such as acquisitions or changes of personnel. It includes information on key buyers and on signals picked up at events with them. Your people need to know about work that is being done at the client by others in the firm and of impending meetings that may yield critical information. The more people and practices you have working at an account, the more complicated this becomes. Management can make this job easier.

Encouraging monthly account meetings is one way of gathering intelligence. This will work well early in the account development process when there are few team members who need to get to know each other, the amount of work being done at the client is limited, and the quantity of information to be shared is small. Later, when account teams and the amount of work being done at a client grows, meetings alone may not be timely enough nor long enough to ensure an adequate flow of information.

Some firms have supplemented meetings with simple tools. For instance, one firm provided a marketing staff member to debrief team members weekly and write a concise memo for each account containing news that team members needed to know.

Sophisticated CRM systems are a more elaborate way of addressing the need. Some systems provide fields for recording the name of the person from your firm who knows each contact at an account as well as information on recent conversations. They automatically send information on meetings at the client and other key events to all members of the account team.

Communication is at the heart of cross selling. Good communication will be more effective, of course, if it is reinforced by your rewards system—the subject of the next chapter.

13

Rewarding Cross Selling

With Alan Johnson

Professionals, like other people, respond to rewards. Unless you compensate people for cross selling, they aren't likely to do it. You must applaud them for doing it, pay them for doing it, promote them for doing it, and give them access to the best clients. If you don't, well, you are likely to get what you pay for. Firm management's willingness to do these things is, to put it bluntly, a test of whether it is serious about getting results. If you don't measure results and reward on the basis of those measurements, you aren't really interested in cross selling. Show me a firm where the cross-selling effort is all talk, and I will show you one where cross selling isn't measured or rewarded.

One professional we interviewed said:

> We are all supposed to cross sell, but cross selling makes little difference in people's compensation or chance of promotion. What really counts in this firm is keeping your people billing. There is a lot of pressure to keep your people busy. So it's hard to capture the attention of someone you want to introduce you into one of their accounts. It's not that they're against doing it. It's simply a

distraction from what really counts. The reward for introducing another practice is so small that it doesn't really do anything for them, and there is always the risk that the client won't like you and that you will mess up their relationship. In this environment, it's hard to get people to cross sell.

That you must reward cross selling doesn't make it easy. There are several problems with setting up rewards systems:

Differences in the ability to cross sell make it hard to set up an equitable system. Some practices are in a much better position to cross sell than others. Auditors, for example, work extremely closely with high-level clients, talking with them about their concerns and issues. They are well positioned to cross sell. Not all practices enjoy their advantages.

Some practices in a firm are also easier to cross sell than others. Some are at the cutting edge of their fields, while others are competent at providing a commodity service.

Given these problems it's impossible to set up a system that rewards effort evenly and provides benefit to everyone.

You risk encouraging short-term sales over long-term relationships. A poorly constructed rewards system will focus your people on making the next sale, rather than protecting and deepening the firm's long-term relationship with a client. This can lead to a "strip-mining mentality," as one strategy consultant aptly put it.

Even the best-planned compensation system won't replace good management oversight. Not all sales should be made, and the selling of work you shouldn't take can be an unintended consequence of your rewards system. The more you reward cross selling, the greater incentive you create to push for sales, good and bad. That means that the more you reward cross selling, the more management oversight is required to quickly stop any inappropriate behaviors.

You risk divisive behavior as your professionals compete for sales credits. A system that measures cross selling implies that such things as leads and introductions are measured and monitored. If one person is clearly responsible, the measurement and subsequent reward are easy. If two people are involved, the issue gets muddy because you have to determine how to allocate credit between them. If three or more people are involved, not only is allocation of credit complicated, the subsequent reward shrinks for each partic- ipant. Also, whether or not a lead or introduction would have come without the benefit of another practice is sometimes unclear.

Once again, your rewards system can have consequences you don't expect. An executive search firm set up a system that was supposed to encourage cross selling by providing credits for introductions and sales assists that were to be used in calculating compensation. Some of the recruiters would sell a piece of work in another practice's area, claim the credits, and then do the searches themselves to capture as much of the fee as possible, even though they weren't best qualified to do the work. This was cross selling gone mad. Management responded by revising the system to disqualify a recruiter from getting any sales credit if he or she did a search in another practice's specialty.

Complicated systems won't work. Solving the preceding problems can induce a firm to set up a complicated rewards system. But complicated systems don't work. A system must be visible and easy to understand. The measurements that underlie it must be simple enough that reporting is easy and results are known promptly, so that people always know how they are doing. Simplicity and clarity are more effective than complexity and obscurity, but they are hard to achieve.

Firms that address these problems realize that over the long haul the ability to cross sell is often a sign that a professional truly has deep and trusting relationships with clients, has strong sales skills, and is a team player, all of which should be rewarded. The ability to cross sell encapsulates many of the traits that most firms want to encourage.

They also realize that once behaviors are measured and rewarded, those behaviors become the focus of interest, conversation, and constructive feedback. They make all conversations about cross selling immediately relevant to the firm's professionals. They are, then, a foundation for an effective cross-selling effort.

There are three basic approaches to designing compensation that motivates and rewards cross selling. The one you select should reflect your firm's underlying compensation system, the culture you want to build, and the nature of the firm's business. In the right environment, all three can work. The primary difference among them is the degree of management discretion in determining compensation.

Discretionary Compensation

Many firms evaluate performance judgmentally, even when there are established measures and objectives. At such firms, cross selling is one factor, usually a subset of a larger revenue target, used to determine bonus size and salary increase. Firms that use this approach effectively set clear expectations at the beginning of the year for performance and potential variation in reward.

For example, in the first year that a professional has a cross-selling target, it is usually kept low, say at $200,000, with a potential for total compensation to vary ± 5 percent based on achievement. In later years, as the professional gains experience at cross selling, expectations and compensation variability increases. This is all done within a discretionary system that requires evaluation of a variety of performance criteria.

Discretionary compensation systems are, by definition, unclear about weights and measures. They can be effective, but only if they are used to rigorously reinforce the behaviors management wants to see. Too often, they aren't. One behavior may be rewarded in a given year and others in later years as management's attention drifts to other issues. This can create a cynical view of management initiatives. At one firm we know, account teams were charged with increasing sales at major clients. The head of one team was approached by a team member, a partner with many years of experience, who asked, "How long do we have to keep at this before we can give up and go back to what we usually do?" A negative person? Maybe. But he was certainly one who had seen many fleeting management initiatives. He had a good sense of what would be rewarded in the long haul, and it wasn't cross selling.

Some general rules for making this kind of system work include:

Make sure it sticks for several years. If you aren't willing to reward people for cross selling for several years, don't start. You can't build and institutionalize cross-selling behaviors within a large firm in a year or two. It requires a focused effort for several years. Though this can be said of all three kinds of reward systems, it is a particular issue with discretionary systems. Because they are *discretionary*, they make it easy for management's focus to shift in response to short-term pressures. If that happens, you will have a hard time institutionalizing cross selling in your firm.

Reward the behaviors you are looking for. Reward people for what you want them to do and what is in their power to do. If a person is in a position to make introductions but not to close sales for other practices, reward her for introductions rather than for business generated. To make sure that the introductions have been of the proper quality, ask for comments from those who have been introduced. This kind of measure provides important insight into whether people have "gotten with the program" long before revenues start to come in.

Move towards rewarding revenue generation as the program matures. Because there is a lag between effort and result in cross selling, it can be wise to bias your rewards toward behaviors at first, when cross-sold revenues are scarce. Over time, as revenues increase, you can move toward rewarding revenues generated.

So, for example, in the first year of a program a firm might expect a partner to provide eight solid cross-selling opportunities and $200,000 in cross-sold revenue, with opportunities and revenues each having a weighting of 50 percent. In that year, total compensation is expected to vary by no more ± 5 percent as influenced by cross selling. In later years, the partner might be compensated solely on revenues generated through cross selling, and her income may be affected by ± 10 percent. Also after the first year, cross-selling effectiveness becomes a factor in promotion and partner selection.

For this kind of program to work, cross-selling activities, like introductions, and cross-selling revenues must be reported promptly and summarized on a simple form. The results should be communicated to program participants at least quarterly.

Schedule-Based Compensation
Firms using this approach evaluate performance in relation to specific objectives. So, for example, 50 percent of a professional's incentive might be earned on performance against a revenue production schedule. In such cases, weightings and values are assigned to cross selling as a part of an explicit compensation program. An average partner might be expected to bring eight significant cross-selling opportunities to others in the firm, which generate at least $200,000 in revenue. (See Exhibit 13.1.) If he achieves that goal, he earns a

specified bonus. If he exceeds or falls short of that goal, his bonus goes up or down in accordance with a specified schedule.

Exhibit 13.1
Sample Schedule-Based Bonus

	Opportunities Generated	Cross-Selling Revenues	Compensation Factor
Target	16 or more	$400,000	20%
	12	$300,000	15%
	8	$200,000	10%
	6	$150,000	7½%
	4 or less	$100,000	5%

Even at firms using this kind of program, management often reserves the right to use moderate discretion to recognize contributions not accounted for by the system.

Linking rewards to a specific schedule of performance makes management commitment to cross selling clear. But clarity is achieved with the sacrifice of flexibility. This can be a problem when, for example, a partner does everything required to cross sell a service into his account, only to have the practice he is introducing turn down the work for lack of resources. Under a rigid application of this approach, the partner would receive no reward for his effort, even though the failure to make a sale rests with the other practice. This is why most systems of this type include escape clauses, allowing management to make judgments in the interests of fairness.

Such systems do force management to clarify expectations about levels and timing of cross selling. This forces management to make a realistic assessment of the potential from cross selling, which can be good for the firm. That assessment is spelled out in the compensation system for everyone to see.

Commission-Based Compensation

Senior professionals can be compensated directly on sales performance by a commission formula with cross selling as one component of the program. For example, you can pay your professionals a commission on sales, say 10 percent on revenue from their own practice areas and 15 percent from cross selling. (See Exhibit 13.2.) Thus, a partner selling $700,000 of business for his own practice and $200,000 for others would earn a commission of $70,000 on the former and $30,000 on the latter. This example assumes that no credit sharing was required.

Exhibit 13.2
Sample Commission-Based Bonus

	Core Revenue	Cross-Sold Revenue
Sales	$700,000	$200,000
x Credit Factor	10%	15%
= Commission	$70,000	$30,000

Though dedicated salespeople are usually paid under this kind of program, it remains an uncommon model for professionals. It is just too hard to determine sales credits and simultaneously retain supportive and cooperative behaviors.

This approach avoids both the need to establish individual goals and the need to make judgments about contribution. Unless carefully administered, however, such systems reduce teamwork as partners compete with each other for sales credit. Also, any professional choosing to ignore the chance for commission may flout the firm's effort to encourage cross selling. Finally, unless your people are used to being paid on commission, installing such a system may jolt the firm's culture; the organization may reject it.

When selecting a compensation approach, you should consider not only the firm's culture, but also the level of urgency you feel about cross selling. Generally, the more explicit the link between cross selling and compensation, the more short-term progress your people will make. In any firm, cross-selling expectations need to be balanced with the maturity of the performance management system. It will do you no good to install a system that requires more specific measurement of cross-selling activity than the firm's reporting systems are capable of providing. In firms where performance discussions are already candid and clear, explicit linkages between cross-selling and compensation can be quite effective. If you have a history of saying you will reward one thing and not exactly doing so, expect it to take time to get your people to believe that you are serious about cross selling, regardless of the compensation system you adopt.

The following story illustrates the importance of emphasizing cross selling in the context of a specific firm:

> The management committee at a large law firm had identified cross selling as key to the firm's growth. The firm's attorneys frequently expressed interest in and support for cross selling, pointing out many conceptual opportunities for it, but management could point to little tangible result. It dealt with the problem with a three-step process. First, the need for cross selling and opportunity to do it were validated, and specific goals and measures were established by practice and geography. Though historically there had been talk about the huge potential to cross sell, goals were modest. During the first year or two of the effort, management wanted all goals to appear readily achievable.

Second, expectations were clearly communicated to the attorneys. A new tracking and crediting system provided monthly reports to senior management. This ensured that the emphasis would be clear and sustained. Partners were asked how they were doing, and they began to talk more concretely about opportunities. They were encouraged to think of areas where the firm had a particularly strong reputation, where making introductions would be easiest.

Finally, management changed the compensation system to incorporate cross-selling performance. This was done within an existing discretionary system.

Results improved significantly. Cross selling became such an ingrained behavior within the firm that the professionals later disavowed that compensation had any role in the change.

Whichever approach you choose, you must have information on cross sales and cross-selling efforts to support compensation decisions. Setting up a reporting system that ensures this information is available when needed usually requires a joint effort of finance, information technology, and human resources departments. Often firms have to start programs with imperfect information and then work quickly to obtain better data as the program unfolds. Without good information, it will be hard for your people to accept that cross selling really affects compensation.

Complicating this issue is the need to split credit for a cross sale among two or more professionals. Some firms do this by allowing double-counting, whereby two people can take credit for the same revenue. These systems are designed to make sure that the firm doesn't pay out more in compensation than the new revenue is worth. At others, revenue credit is simply split according to established guidelines, say 20 percent of the credit going to the person who makes the introduction, 20 percent for the person or people who make the sale, 10 percent for support on proposal writing and related activities, and 50 percent to those who deliver the work. Some firms have developed five or six typical splits to illustrate the guidelines. Typically, management makes the call on who gets what portion of the credit based on input from the participants.

Unless your people are paid to cross sell, many of them won't. Any rewards system you employ to encourage cross selling must be suitable within the culture of your firm. Whatever system you chose, it must be a clear statement of management's focused attention on cross selling. You have to let your people know that you are serious.

14

Cross-Selling Failures

Though the concepts associated with cross selling are simple, execution is difficult, especially when a professional must fit it into days that are already packed with client work and internal meetings. Both the client organization and the professional's own firm can be large and complex, leaving plenty of room for confusion and error. Even intelligent and capable people sometimes fail at cross selling. And we can learn from their misfortunes.

In the course of our research, we collected many examples of cross-selling failures. These stories can provide lessons, though we must use them with caution for several reasons. First, we did not collect these stories in as much detail as we did the success stories because the professionals we interviewed were usually less comfortable in relating them. Also, we received only one person's perspective on each of these failures, and none of us can be completely objective about emotionally charged experiences such as these.

Still, the stories are instructive. I suggest that you read and reflect on each story, trying to come up with your own interpretation, before you read the analysis that follows it.

All Talk and No Action

Our firm identified accounts that it wanted to target and assigned teams to each of them. Some of the teams have done well. For example, one team developed an account over four years from no revenue to a total of $20 million. Others haven't had any success. There are several reasons for this. Some have faced heavily entrenched competition, for example. But many have failed because they simply don't *do* anything. They meet and everyone talks about things they *could* do or *might* do, and then they don't follow through. A month later they get together and have another meeting much like the one before.

Analysis

This is a common problem. If you never talk to a buyer, you will never sell anything. You must find ways to meet buyers and then to remain in touch with them to develop the relationship. Professionals who are successful at cross selling meet with buyers regularly. In terms of our model, they manage the cross-selling process by having events. Any account team that goes a month without having an event of some kind with a buyer at the target company should know that its efforts are stymied. If it goes two months without an event, its efforts are probably dead.

In this example, senior management of the firm had also not communicated that cross selling was a priority.

Weak Internal Relationships

We were doing a replacement study for one hospital in a twelve-hospital system. In a task force meeting at the client, we uncovered a huge logistical issue that resulted in high inventory cost: There was no information system that would warn the purchasing department about an impending out-of-stock situation. As a result, the hospitals had to overstock most items to make sure they always had supplies when they needed them.

We have real gurus in this kind of issue in other parts of the organization. But try as we might, we couldn't get a supply chain management project. The people in that practice weren't ready to help us. They weren't as comfortable with health care clients as with other industries where they had more experience. We couldn't identify who in our own organization we should talk to. When we finally identified a person, three meetings were canceled before we actually talked. Then we tried to arrange a time for someone to come out to see the client but were told that everyone was so busy that they couldn't come right now. However, the client wanted to talk *now*.

We just couldn't put it together before we finished our project. Now we aren't working for the client anymore and making it happen will be all that much harder.

Analysis

Difficulty working within one's own organization was the most common kind of cross-marketing failure described and the most laden with emotion.

In this case, the relationships between the speaker and the people in the supply chain practice were not strong when the opportunity arose to cross sell. Had the participants better anticipated the potential to cross sell and built better personal relationships between the two practices before an opportunity arose, either on their own or as a part of an institutional effort, the problems described might well have been avoided. The representative of the health care practice would have known immediately who to turn to. That person would already have committed support to a cross-selling effort. The speaker would have better understood if the opportunity was likely to be attractive to the supply chain practice and how to promote it internally. It is hard to cross sell with someone with whom you have no prior relationship.

Knowing When to Take a Pass

A plastic injection molding company was growing like crazy and looking to replace their auditor. I started pursuing the audit in March, knowing that a decision would be made in December. I got to know the chairman, who had built the place on his marketing ability; he was a strong-willed guy. We got along pretty well, and he told me that he planned to give us the audit and asked if we could do an organizational study of his business. He wanted an assessment of the whole enterprise.

I didn't think we did this kind of work but sent out an e-mail and got a response from a partner who had the expertise and interest in building a practice there. I personally took him out to talk with the chairman about the organizational study. They got into an argument over how the work should be done. I'd never seen anything like it. I literally had to be the referee. The chairman would suggest that we do a part of the work in a specific way, and the partner would say, no, he couldn't do it that way; it had to be done his way.

The next morning I got a call from the chairman saying it wouldn't work because the partner was too committed to his methodology. He also said that when it came to the audit, he would not be interested in anyone who worked in the office with that partner. So we had lost ground on the audit. Needless to say, I never referred work to that partner again. These weren't technical deficiencies; they were issues of inflexibility. The partner wasn't sophisticated enough to be involved in cross selling.

Six months later when the chairman called to talk about the audit, I brought in a seasoned partner and a young dynamic audit partner from a different office. I knew them both well and we got the audit.

Analysis

The one orchestrating the account was in a difficult position. If he had passed on the opportunity to do the assessment, some other firm would have gotten the work and been in a position to win the audit as well. So he was under strong pressure to find someone who could address the client's concern. He tried introducing someone he hardly knew, once again showing that it pays to have a relationship with the people you are going to cross sell with before you try to cross sell together. That way you can sort out in advance who you are willing to take to a client meeting and who you are not. In this case, had he known the partner in question better, he might well have decided to take a pass on the introduction.

As we have seen in earlier chapters, there are many things that management can do to encourage professionals in a firm to get to know each other. But any professional who wants to cross sell should take it upon himself or herself to learn about the services and personal characteristics of others in the firm. That knowledge is essential to effective cross selling.

The Wrong Account Manager

A former client called us and told us that a company they were invested in was facing bankruptcy. From a legal perspective, there were bankruptcy, intellectual property, and corporate issues. Unfortunately, this opportunity arose when the whole firm was busy with other work. I pulled in a bankruptcy partner because the initial issue was how to protect the client if the other company filed for bankruptcy. He really knew bankruptcy law, and I was swamped on other matters so I didn't pay much attention to the issue until the client called and said that his boss, the general counsel, was unhappy.

Our partner handling the account was technically knowledgeable, but the client wanted someone to take charge and help set strategy and show them options—someone to stay three or four steps ahead of them. Our partner wasn't doing that. He wasn't giving the sense that he was planning to deal with the next problem that would come up in a few days. It turned out that this partner was really busy, too, and simply wasn't able to devote the time. I asked another partner, who was a real take-charge kind of guy, to take over the account, even though he was a real estate attorney by training. He became the strategist and let the bankruptcy guy do his work.

Analysis

This story has a twist because bankruptcy attorneys often understand clients' broad business issues better than other kinds of lawyers do. In this case, however, the real estate attorney was the better account manager. The story suggests that the client was eager for someone to sell them a vision of the total solution and that the bankruptcy attorney was unable to do so. In addition to failing to keep the client happy, the bankruptcy attorney was likely missing opportunities to provide additional services.

Missing a Buyer and Having Unclear Value

We were doing a lot of work with a meat packer. The meat industry operates on razor-thin margins and is operationally oriented. Management often makes decisions based on gut feelings. If you buy the wrong cows or process them wrong or make some other mistake, every penny per pound you lose is worth $50 million. The situation is complex because the decisions are interrelated.

We didn't do a good enough job early on of showing that the analytical approach we provided, as opposed to their heuristic approach, was valuable to them. We couldn't show that they made more money because we had helped them set up an analytical system. It wasn't evident to them that we would be instrumental to their success going forward.

I had an okay but not great relationship with the president of the division. Then he got promoted to the corporate office. The new president of the division had been head of operations and was a nuts-and-bolts kind of guy. He hadn't been involved in the genesis of the project.

He just didn't get it, but he realized that, gee, these guys were expensive. I didn't spend the time necessary with him to get him educated.

Analysis

The speaker has a good grasp of the problem. In the terms of the BEST Selling Model, he didn't have enough events to develop a strong relationship with people who turned out to be key buyers. Had he been able to develop a strong business case and to sell a vision of the impact of the work to them, the firm might still be working at this client.

Missing a buyer is another common cross-selling failure.

The Need for Goal Alignment

A client called me with a process-engineering project on a wastewater issue. This isn't my specialty, so I asked a chemical engineer with the right qualifications to manage it. Not long after that, the client called me and said he wouldn't work with this person. He was still willing to work with our firm, but not with this specific project manager. The project was over budget and behind schedule, and the client wasn't likely to implement the recommendations the project team was making. They were too esoteric for that client. This project manager didn't realize that you have to tailor your recommendations for the specific client. He was technically focused and got excited about an approach that was too capital intensive for this client.

We lost a lot of trust as a result of this problem. Now I have to rebuild confidence and we will be back in a quasi-competitive mode when this client has more work. I was busy and didn't stay close enough to the project.

Analysis

As the account manager would probably agree, this example makes a good case for close project management. It shows why an account manager who really understands the client can add value at meetings outside his or her specialty. These people belong at major client and internal meetings that deal with issues of importance to their accounts. Among their most important responsibilities is keeping the firm's work aligned with the client's goals, something that didn't happen in this case.

The Weakest Link

We had been working at a software company in one of its divisions and the CEO asked us to meet with the head of the health care division, which developed software for the health care industry. I knew another key player in that division, too, so when I was invited in, I thought we were sure to get some business.

I brought along a consultant from our health care group who knew the health care arena better than I did and who had actually sold computer systems to doctors' offices. I decided to give her a lead role in the meeting, believing that with my relationship and her expertise we would make a sale.

I had worked with her for five years and knew her, but didn't realize that she hadn't been in front of a CEO before. She was intimidated and didn't live up to her billing in the client's eyes as an expert in the health field. She wasn't aggressive or proactive in the meeting. Her overall presentation was flat and not compelling. So we didn't get any work with that division. I should have prepared her better.

It turned out that the head of the division didn't like consultants and didn't like the CEO or anyone else mucking around in his business. He was looking for a reason not to use us. He went back to the CEO and said he didn't like my colleague, and the CEO had to agree. I should have realized that I had the relationship with the CEO and that I would have to work to transfer relationships to the division head. Trying to transfer it to someone else in our firm before I had built my own relationship with the division head was extremely risky.

At later meetings at other clients that I went to with this same colleague, we changed roles and were successful.

Analysis

Each time you meet a new buyer, the relationship building must start all over again. As noted earlier in this book, you can never just give a relationship to someone else. Yet, in essence, that is what the speaker tried to do. The speaker's colleague had no relationship with the head of the division, the person with whom she would work and be accountable to, had the firm won the assignment. This was a weak link to base a sale on when a stronger one was available.

Taking Your Lumps

The audit partner at an automobile supplier referred us in to do some work. I was surprised because he was the doubting type who never brought anyone else into one of his accounts. It turned out that he had learned that the client was considering using a Big Five firm to do some work and we were the lesser of two evils.

We did a few hundred thousand dollars worth of work, which the client liked. The work raised some additional questions, and he asked for some additional analyses and reports. Before we had even scoped it out with the client, the partner said he wanted us to do it for free. I said, "Let's go out and find out what they want before we give it away. If it is the right size, we can give it away, but we don't know what we're looking at here yet."

He ignored this advice and put his arm around the client and said he would take care of him and promised it for free. It turned out that that free work destroyed the profitability of all the previous work. This is the kind of outcome that hurts the whole process because it makes people question whether they want to take the risk of getting into this kind of situation.

Analysis

It doesn't pay to cross sell with someone who doesn't want it to be a win for everyone, the client and all practices involved. To the account manager's credit, he didn't renege on doing the work but looked after the client's interests first and learned a valuable lesson. He lost profits, taking his lumps on this one.

An Unclear Agenda

Several weeks ago we gave a presentation to the CEO and his senior staff at [an electronic equipment manufacturer]. It was on the life cycle of products, something we didn't think they managed well. It was a valuable presentation, and everyone applauded at the end. At one point the CEO asked the presenter if what we talked about would be hard to do. He wanted to know how long it would take to do it alone. The presenter said that if we were to help it would take about a month, and I heard the CEO whisper to the head of the business unit that he hadn't realized they were getting a sales pitch. This wasn't a sales presentation, but one remark turned it into a sales pitch in his mind. It was a passing remark, but it didn't help us. This shows how important it is to try to help your clients, to keep their interests in mind, and take the leap of faith that good things will follow.

Analysis

It also shows that having clarity about the agenda for every client meeting is essential. All of the team members must understand what the agenda is and realize that no one has a right to change the agenda, except the client. A free, value-added presentation should not be a disguised sales pitch, no matter how much you hope the client will want to hire you to do work in the area. Unless the client raises the subject, you should not try to sell your services at such an event.

Lost Relationships

I used to be the account manager for a big food products company that merged with another firm. I had known everyone there, and we did $8 million to $9 million of work there a year. They would ask us for help, so we seldom had to sell very hard. The merger turned into a reverse takeover. Our friends were out, and the leadership team from the other company was in. A competitor had very good relations with the new management team. As a result, our revenues dropped precipitously, even though we offer a broader range of services.

Analysis

There may not be much the account manager could have done to avoid this problem. It shows that even when you are doing most things right, you can lose an account.

Difficulty Displacing Another Professional

I litigate insurance coverage matters for large corporations. I was so successful with one client that they threw a party for me and introduced me to several of their executives. But it's been a bear getting other business from them even though I know they want to give it to me. They are happy with the work being done for them by their other attorneys. A lot of their product liability cases are low-end work that they get attorneys willing to charge $90 per hour to work on. They just haven't had another case in New Jersey that I can handle, and they won't give us the corporate work.

Analysis

There are two possible assessments of this situation. First, the professional may have picked a poor account to target for more work. There may never be significant opportunities at this account. Alternatively, he may simply need more patience. If he waits and keeps up his relationships with the people he knows at the account, one of the attorneys he competes with may fall out of favor or may have a conflict in a case. Then he might get the chance he is looking for.

We must weigh our willingness to invest in the pursuit of an account against the likelihood of that client ever hiring the firm for an array of services. There is too little information in the story to give us an answer. But the way the story is told suggests that the professional may not be asking himself this key question.

Enemies That Get You Later

The people in one business unit wanted to work with us because they didn't feel that the corporate marketing people cared enough or were qualified to do a good job for them. Looking back, this sense on the part of the client resulted from the 5 percent problem—the unit we were working with accounted for only 5 percent of the company's revenues and so didn't get much attention from the corporate marketing staff. But we took the business unit people at their word and didn't treat the corporate marketing people like clients. We had only one good contact there and when he left things got kind of hostile.

Part of the problem was pride on our part. We felt that we were dealing with the head of the business unit and other leaders of that team. Why should we have to check with the marketing staff? This behavior was short-sighted. That rift has taken us years to heal at the cost of not doing projects for the mother ship. We got the reputation of being renegades. The marketing department only worked with us when they were told to, and then unwillingly.

We were invited to do a presentation on a $350,000 campaign but were one of four firms competing for the business. We didn't get it. Had we managed our relationship with the marketing department better, that could have been a sole-sourced assignment.

Analysis

It seldom pays to make enemies within an account. That staffer who seems so unimportant today may become a key buyer in the future. Staffers tend to have long memories and in many small ways can help or hurt professionals who work with their companies, even if they don't have hiring power. It's worth a little time to develop a relationship with them.

To the speaker's credit, there is no attempt to duck responsibility. This person learned a lesson and will do better next time.

The Need for a Short Rope of Accountability

We had worked with a large municipality on wastewater projects since 1980. Because of the good experience they had had with us, they hired us to help them set up a computer tracking system to ease the reporting to state agencies. We showed them that we had had success automating manual systems so that lab results went straight into the computer.

Our regional office sold the work, but was counting on support from corporate where this expertise resided. We underestimated the complexity of the work when we sold it. Computer people like to tweak things a lot. We didn't bid enough to allow for this, and the project came in over budget and behind schedule. Corporate didn't provide all the resources that were needed because as a firm we were overcommitted. Finally, we did deliver.

This project hurt us with the client and with others in the region because word gets out. This kind of thing can easily happen when a regional office isn't familiar with the service it is selling and relies on the corporate office for backup. Now we transfer someone from headquarters or hire someone locally to serve as a liaison with the corporate team. Corporate, of course, gets nervous that the regional office will build its own capability and not send work back.

Analysis

It sounds as if the people who performed the work on this

project had little hand in designing the budget. Also, those with primary responsibility for client satisfaction did not control the resources required to do the work. Better project management procedures might have avoided many of the problems described in this story.

When Client's Interests Don't Come First

[One of the largest corporations in the world] wanted some work done that would require a team working in every major location they had around the world. We wanted to put together a team, but the unit [from one large European country] said that they were too busy to participate. We tried to put people from elsewhere in the firm into [the country] to work on the project, but they wouldn't let us do it. They said that only their people could work in their country. Of course, they had a lot of reasons why this was so, and because of the way the firm was organized at the time they could enforce it. The work went to our biggest competitor.

After that, the firm was reorganized so that kind of thing couldn't happen again.

Analysis

Someone at this firm failed to put the client's interest first, the firm's second, and their own interests and those of their regional practice only third. Firm management dealt with the problem appropriately by changing policy, making sure that such behavior would be unlikely to succeed in the future.

Not every effort to cross sell your firm's services will work. Rainmakers pick themselves up from a failure and go on to win the next one . . . or the one after that. Each time they lose, they learn something that increases their chances of winning the next time. I hope these examples of unsuccessful attempts to cross sell have shortened that learning process.

15

Ethics and Cross Selling

Cross selling sometimes poses ethical problems, which are best faced and managed. These problems result from the potential conflict between the need to maintain professional objectivity and place the client's interests first and the pressure to sell additional services. A number of large firms have been sued by clients who felt that their interests have not been well looked after by professionals eager to sell the next piece of work,[1] and some of these plaintiffs have collected large sums. The big accounting firms face the threat of increased regulation and as of this writing have all agreed to divest consulting operations because of perceived conflicts of interest. Regulators argue that the objectivity of their audits have sometimes been compromised by the need to please clients with whom the firms have large consulting projects. Brought to a head by the Enron scandal, it is a long-standing issue.[2]

Even before the Enron case, the Securities and Exchange Commission fined an accounting firm $7 million in settlement of a fraud case in light of the way the firm had handled the audit of a large client. In addition to the audit, the firm had provided the client with many millions of dollars of other services. Though the audit team had noted the client's questionable accounting practices and recommended that they be changed, the client had ignored the advice and the accountants had signed off on the audit with unqualified opinions. When the company's poor performance could no longer be concealed, its stock price plummeted. The SEC noted that the top audit partner on the account also served as marketing director for his office, coordinating the cross selling of consulting services and receiving compensation from nonaudit services that were cross sold. This was all publicly reported.[3]

Problems are not confined to the accounting and consulting professions. The built environment industry (architectural, engineering, and construction services) is currently moving toward design/build contracts, in which one entity, usually a construction firm, has responsibility for designing and building a facility by a specific date at a preset fee. But most clients still choose to set up an adversarial relationship between architect and contractor in hopes that architects and contractors will prevent each other from doing things against the clients' interests. Clients often see having the architectural, engineering, and construction contracts held by one firm as too cozy.

Today some accountants not only give their clients investment advice, but also sell the financial instruments they recommend. Big accounting firms are buying up law firms in Europe and hope to do the same in the United States in the future. Some law firms in the United States now have subsidiaries offering a range of services from the traditional lobbying to environmental consulting to money management.[4] Hardware and software vendors operate consulting arms. Consulting firms run outsourcing organizations and sell software products. These changes increase the potential for conflicts of interest.

At the same time, they show that clients often want to go to one provider for multiple services. In other words, cross selling is often a good thing for a client because it often makes sense to buy multiple services from one firm. Clients recognize this and want the opportunity to do so. As Steve Vernon of Watson Wyatt Worldwide notes:

> I've had clients say that all the other firms they work with were cross selling to them, but we weren't. They thought we weren't interested in them. The first time I heard that it was the nail in the coffin to any reluctance I felt.

There are many examples of cases where a client may benefit from hiring one firm instead of two. Clients who hire separate strategy and implementation consulting firms often find there are large gaps between the two services and that the strategy does not always fit with practical reality. The implementation firms almost always feel that they have to redo parts of the strategy to fill these gaps and charge the clients for the work. Clients may argue, with reason, that if both strategy and implementation are done by the same firm, any holes in the strategy are the consultant's problem, not theirs. An analogous case can be made for having:

- All legal services required during an acquisition be provided by one firm.
- A firm's auditors also provide some kinds of consulting services.
- Both architectural and engineering designs for a new building done by one firm.

Here, I argue neither for a client buying all its services from one provider nor for the client distributing them among several. Rather, I suggest that clients should be aware of the potential benefits and pitfalls of both approaches.

Among the potential pitfalls that buyers should be aware of is the risk of ethically questionable behavior that can occur when one professional firm refers business to another. That there is a potential bias when a professional refers someone else in his own firm is obvious. But biases can also exist when there is no opportunity to cross sell, and these can be more pernicious to the client, as they are hidden. Clients often ask their professionals for referrals to someone who can help solve a problem. The narrower the scope of a firm's services, then, the less cross selling it is likely to do and the more third-party referrals it is likely to make. Receiving a referral creates an obligation, and sometimes pressure, to return the favor. This give and take is the origin of powerful referral networks within the professions. These referrals are usually made with the client's best interests in mind, but it isn't always that simple.

A few years ago, a law firm recommended some consultants to turn around one of its clients, a troubled retailer. Later, when the CEO became dissatisfied with the consultants' work and tried to fire them, the lawyers went over his head to the board to argue for their retention. When the board insisted that the consultants stay on, the CEO resigned. His replacement later filed for bankruptcy and sued the consultants for bad advice. During the suit a letter from the law firm to the consulting firm surfaced, which asked for special consideration in referrals because of the services the lawyers had provided on the consultants' behalf in this case. Whatever the facts about the quality of the consulting services provided, the letter showed how referral networks can place pressure on both giver and receiver that is not always transparent to clients.

For many years, some accountants have accepted referral fees from financial advisors. Clients were often unaware of the monetary interest of the accountants in making the referrals. Similarly, many technology consultants have accepted referral fees from hardware and software vendors. At least when one practice in a firm refers business to another within the same firm, the financial benefit to the referrer is implied by the relationship.

Certainly, potential conflicts of interest in making referrals are not confined to cross selling. Still, none of this eliminates the potential for ethically dubious behavior when professionals cross sell. Though professionals don't need to feel defensive about cross selling, they do need to carefully manage the ethical issues inherent in the process. One way to do this is to pose a series of questions that every professional involved in cross selling should consider from time to time:

Are we placing the client's interests and our need for professional disinterest first and the need to cross sell second?

This is, of course, the basic issue and one we have seen before in earlier chapters. It is so fundamental that it bears repeating here. We all need to ask ourselves this question frequently. The remaining questions are simply elaborations or refinements.

As Mike Palmer says:

> The first thing you must always ask yourself is what is best for the client. Get that answer right and you will always have a happy client. That doesn't always get you money tomorrow. [A big investment bank] asked us to do several things that we could have done, but we suggested that they use their auditors, who could handle the job better and cheaper. Don't do anything that will diminish the long-run effort. It can take years to build a relationship and only a few seconds to screw it up.

Of course, you can't put the client's interests first unless you know who the client is. Is the top management of the company the client for an audit, the board, or the investors? A strong case can be made that it is the investors, even though they neither select the auditor nor pay directly for the service. But a consulting service to integrate a large software package, sold by a different practice of the auditor's firm, may have a different client: the CIO, the CFO, or the COO. In that case, the buyer both selects and pays for the firm that will provide the service. In such a complex environment, it's easy to get confused about who the client is . . . at your peril. This is the crux of the problem faced by accounting firms that also provide consulting services.

Is the message that the client's interests and the firm's objectivity come first as loud and clear as the message that the firm wants to cross sell?

On an airplane I once sat next to the CIO of a rapidly growing mortgage company and asked him how he liked his current technology consultants. His words capture the concerns that clients have about the self-serving manner of some professionals and specifically about cross selling. He said:

> They put inexperienced people on my project and expect me to pay for their education. They seem more interested in getting the next job than in doing the current one right. They just want my money.

I doubt the consultants at the well-known firm he referred to view themselves in such mercenary terms, and I can only speculate on what happened to earn such censure. That speculation suggests how hard it can be to place clients' interests ahead of one's own.

Certainly, no one ever told the consultants working on the project that selling more services was more important than doing the current work well. I am sure that firm management would state clearly that, above all else, it is committed to doing high-quality work for its clients. Still, with their behavior the consultants somehow communicated to the client the overarching need to sell more work.

This may be because a similar message was communicated

inside the firm, albeit unintentionally. I believe this often happens because firm management assumes that everyone knows that clients' interests and ethical behavior come first. They say little on the subject but, on the other hand, do speak loudly about the need to cross sell.

Most professional firms are under relentless pressure to produce more revenue. They translate this pressure into rewards systems. Ethical behavior is assumed, but professionals are told that bonuses, raises, and promotions hinge on their ability to sell more work. Reward systems speak loudly about what management wants. Unless firm management administers reward systems carefully, this broad revenue pressure will be converted into pressure on specific clients to buy more work. Pressure sales tactics seldom work in the professions, and if they succeed in the short term are likely to come back and bite the professional later during the relationship with a client. To avoid this problem, all reward systems should include a component for client satisfaction that weighs in before the component for short-term revenue generation.

The greater the need for revenue gets, the more critical it is for management to reiterate that clients' interests come first. Hunger spoils your judgment. It is when you most need work that you are most likely to push too hard to get it or to take work that you shouldn't.

If you are a professional at a firm that takes ethical shortcuts to get work, do not succumb to this behavior yourself. Look for another job.

If there were no additional work at stake for the firm, would I make the same recommendation?

The answer to this question should always be yes. That is easily said, but not so easy in practice. I believe that few professionals get into ethical problems by blatant lies and misrepresentations. Rather, under pressure they shave a judgment. Yes, the best answer may be X, but a case can be made for X-1. The client wants X-1 (and I have a $2 million proposal outstanding), so I will accept the case they make. More specifically, the client has some accounting practices that are questionable but makes a case that it is cleaning up its act, so I will give an unqualified opinion of the audit just this once. It is a slippery slope.

Am I being pressured by the client or a colleague to do something that is against my better judgment and, if so, am I doing the right thing, whatever the impact on my ability to sell more work?

The pressure can be intense and often there is little short-term reward for resisting pressure and doing the right thing. But in the end, pleasing the client or a colleague in the short term is not worth the price of your reputation for professional disinterest.

Keep in mind that you want to work at an account for many years to come. Responding to immediate pressure with a short-term ethical compromise may seem to make that more likely. But should your ethics ever be questioned, you are likely to be excluded from the account forever. Some of the most important decisions we make are what assignments *not* to accept.

How would I feel if my behavior and recommendations were reported in the media?

This is a good test. If you wouldn't want to read about it in the newspaper, you probably shouldn't do it. An auditor who is reluctant to provide an unqualified sign-off on a client's financial statements, but who is under pressure to do so, would be wise to ask himself this question.

Is it clear when you are selling versus when you are advising?

Professionals also get into ethical trouble when they mix

advising and selling. The clearer it is when you are advising and when you are selling, the more comfortable a client is likely to be with your efforts to sell more work. Sometimes this can be done presumptively because you know that the client knows you are selling. Sometimes you can make the transition from advising to selling with a simple statement, like "That is something we could help you with, if you would like to talk about it." Sometimes more elaborate wording is required, like "These are some of the things you need to do to deal with this issue. We could help you with them, but I would only want to talk about that if you were sure you didn't want to do it yourself. My primary interest is that the problem gets taken care of properly and if a little time now would help you do that, I would be happy to give it. How do you want to proceed?" This kind of language helps ensure that the client never feels blindsided by a sales pitch when she thought she was getting objective advice.

A clear distinction between advising and selling is particularly important when a professional makes claims about the superiority of someone he is referring to a client. When I worked at a large organization, a senior member of another service team recommended that I refer him to a client by saying that I had carefully researched the field and objectively determined that his organization was the best in the business. That he was asking me to lie about having conducted such research didn't bother him. Nor was he impressed by my concern that the client might doubt my claim of objectivity when referring someone else from my firm. I was willing to say that I thought my client needed the service and that my colleagues were excellent in this area and would be easy to work with. All this was true. A little hyperbole is expected when you are selling—clients want to work with people who have confidence in their own organizations. But trying to mask a positive feeling about your own organization as objective advice will quickly undermine a client's confidence in you.

Of course, you can extol someone in a way that is both credible and truly objective. You can recommend the client use a firm other than your own. Once you have demonstrated your willingness to put the client's interest first this way, your claims of the superiority of your firm's services in other areas will be more believable. A number of the people we interviewed for this book mentioned this point. Says Mike Peters, at the time of this interview of Price waterhouseCoopers:

> Sometimes you have to refer a competitor because you don't have the time or the right expertise. It's less risky if the competitor already has an in at the client. It's also a good way to build credibility, especially if the firm is going to surface as a competitor anyway. Of course this can backfire, but you have little choice. You have to be honest with people.

Is the client willing to be cross sold?

If the client is unwilling to be cross sold, she may interpret your efforts to do so ungenerously. From a practical perspective, it is usually a waste of time to try to sell something to someone who doesn't want to buy.

Some companies have a policy of distributing work among several firms. They tend to be meticulous about the ability of the professionals who service them to maintain objectivity at all times. They don't want the close relationships with professionals that is inherent in cross selling. If you have such a client, serve them the way they want to be served. Overstrenuous efforts to cross sell may be misinterpreted.

Does the client know what value she can expect to receive from each assignment I sell?

You will also find yourself in ethical trouble if the client believes he or she is buying one thing and gets another. When you are selling, you want the client to have a clear idea of what she is buying. If the service you are selling now is only one step in a larger process that may require additional services, you want the client to know that early in the selling process. This is the strength of selling an integrated solution. When a professional sells a vision of an integrated solution, he makes clear the full set of services is required and, in turn, the value they will provide to the client. If there are uncertainties about exactly what services will be needed, he spells that out, too, giving the client a sense of the range of possibilities. This done, the client is unlikely to feel misused later when the professional suggests additional work. But if a client agrees to pay you a fee to solve a problem and learns later that additional fees will be required to really get it solved (e.g., to get value she expected to get from the first piece of work you sold her), she may well feel abused.

If we establish clear ethical expectations for our people and ourselves, our chances of avoiding the ethical hazards of cross selling are greater than if we simply assume that everyone will do what is right and rely on good judgment alone.

Cross selling doesn't happen without nurturing. It would be nice to think that ethical behavior does. But it is dangerous to do so.

16
Conclusion

The more services our firms offer and the more that the industries we serve consolidate, the greater the need to cross sell. The bigger our clients grow, the greater the opportunity. Management of many of the firms we work with realize that future growth is far more likely to come from cross selling than from tapping new markets. The argument for cross selling is compelling.

But cross selling is hard. It's not conceptually hard; the concepts presented in this book are all quite simple. It's hard to execute. Why? Because success depends on a personal commitment by many individual professionals supported by institutional resources, programs, and systems. Getting all those people to coordinate their efforts is difficult. It's hard to execute because the individual professionals are already struggling with heavy workloads. Cross selling must somehow be squeezed into overfilled schedules. It's hard because it requires everybody's focused attention over years, not just months, and that is as challenging for management as it is for the individual professional.

But the firms that succeed will develop such powerful positions with their clients that competitors will find it difficult to dislodge them. The more work you do at a client, the more people you know there, the more events you attend, and the more signals you get. This means that the more work you do at a client, the more opportunities you get to sell still more work. Unless a smaller competitor has a strong niche or unusual relationship with the client, it gets squeezed out. Some firms already see this at their large accounts.

The BEST Selling Model provides a means for cross selling that is simple and easy to remember, flexible and adaptable to varying marketing conditions, and practical because it is action-oriented. Our research tells us that successful rainmakers apply something very much like it to build cross selling into their weekly routines. And they get results. It is my hope that those who learn from this book and apply the model will find the job of cross selling a little easier and more rewarding.

Notes

Introduction

1. Linowitz, Sol M. with Martin Mayer. 1994. *The Betrayed Profession: Lawyering at the End of the Twentieth Century.* Baltimore: The Johns Hopkins Press, pp. 22–23.

Raisel, Ethan M., *The McKinsey Way.* 1998. New York: McGraw-Hill, pp. 49–50.

2. Maister, David H. 1997. *True Professionalism: The Courage to Care About Your People, Your Clients and Your Career.* New York: The Free Press, pp. 178–179.

Chapter 1

1. Klein, Gary. 1998. *Sources of Power: How People Make Decisions.* Cambridge: The MIT Press.

Chapter 2

1. I am indebted for this term to the people at The Alexander Group.

2. Miller, Robert B. and Stephen E. Heiman with Tad Tuleja. 1985. *Strategic Selling: The Unique Sales Approach Proven Successful by America's Best Companies.* New York: Warner Books.

Heiman, Stephen E. and Diane Sanchez with Tad Tulega.

1998. *The New Strategic Selling: The Unique Sales Approach Proven Successful by the World's Best Companies.* New York: Warner Books.

Chapter 3

1. For a discussion of this subject, see Cialdini, Robert B. 2001. *Influence: Science and Practice.* Needham Heights, MA: Allyn and Bacon, pp. 52–97. The subject is also addressed briefly in Peters, Thomas J. and Robert H. Waterman, Jr. 1982. *In Search of Excellence: Lessons from America's Best Run Companies.* New York: Warner Books, p. 74.

2. Caplan, Lincoln. 1993. *Skadden: Power, Money, and the Rise of a Legal Empire.* New York: Farrar Straus Giroux, pp. 81–86.

Chapter 4

1. I recommend the following books on this subject:

Heiman, Stephen E. and Diane Sanchez with Tad Tulega. 1998. *The New Strategic Selling: The Unique Sales Approach Proven Successful by the World's Best Companies. op. cit.* This book helps the readers analyze complex sales, sales made over many meetings to several buyers. Key to the authors' approach is understanding the different kinds of buyers one is likely to face. My categorization of buyers is somewhat different because I am writing specifically about cross selling.

Maister, David H., Charles H. Green and Robert M. Galford. 2000. *The Trusted Advisor.* New York: The Free Press. This book provides excellent guidance on how to build trusted-advisor relationships with clients.

Parninello, Anthony. 1994. *Selling to VITO, the Very Important Top Officer.* Avon, MA: Adams Media Corporation. This book describes a cold-calling approach in a style that is a bit in-your-face for most professionals. It has valuable material for those willing to get beyond the hard-selling prose, including insights into buyers.

Sheth, Jagdish and Andrew Sobel. 2000. *Clients for Life: How Great Professionals Develop Breakthrough Relationships.* New York: Simon & Schuster. This book deals with the same subject as the preceding one from a somewhat different perspective.

My previous books also deal extensively with relationship-building with clients. Harding, Ford. 1998. *Creating Rainmakers, The Manager's Guide to Training Professionals to Attract New Clients.* Avon, MA: Adams Media Corporation, pp. 131–148; Harding, Ford. 1994. *Rain Making, The Professional's Guide to Attracting New Clients.* Avon, MA: Adams Media Corporation, pp. 43–59 and 73–87.

I have discussed the power of large networks in my previous book:

Harding, Ford. 1998. *Creating Rainmakers: The Manager's Guide to Training Professionals to Attract New Clients. op. cit.* p. 19–27. After this book was published, I learned that the relationship it describes is known as Metcalfe's Law. For a description of this law, see Downes, Larry and Chunka Mui. 1998. *Unleashing the Killer App: Digital Strategies for Market Dominance.* Boston: Harvard Business School Press, pp. 23–28.

Chapter 5

1. For a good discussion of brainstorming techniques see the book by IDEO's managing director Kelly, Tom with Jonathan Littman. 2001. *The Art of Innovation.* New York: Currency/ Doubleday, pp. 53–66.

Chapter 6

1. Carey, Susan and Scott McCartney. April 20, 2001. "Flying Lessons: With TWA, American Plots Course to Avoid Airline Merger Pitfalls," the *Wall Street Journal,* pp. A1 and A10.

2. Anonymous, 1988. *A Vision of Grandeur.* Chicago. This is the official history of the accounting firm now know as Andersen.

I also appreciate the help provided by Eugene Delves for insights into cross selling at this firm in its earlier years. Delves was one of the original five members of a task force created to study the possible use of computers in business and so was arguably one of the first five computer consultants in the world. He tells of how he entered the field when, as a young accountant, he was called to the managing partner's office late one Friday. There the managing partner and another senior partner offered him an opportunity to work on a project at Commonwealth Edison. There was a mock computer (actually just a binary counter) in the room to illustrate the then unbelievable speed of computing. It had many flashing cathode-ray tubes. Delves was told that he didn't have to take the assignment and that he could take some time to decide but to get back to them before the day was out. When he went home that night he told his parents that he thought he had made a career change and he believed it had something to do with light bulbs.

Chapter 7

1. Rackham, Neil. 1988. *SPIN Selling.* New York: McGraw-Hill.

2. I am indebted for this term to the people at The Alexander Group.

Chapter 8

1. For a discussion of tipping points, see Gladwell, Malcolm. 2000. *The Tipping Point: How Little Things Can Make a Big Difference.* Boston: Little, Brown & Company. This book discusses how fads are created. It has relevance to cross selling because, in essence, we want our services to become fads at major accounts.

Chapter 9

1. I am indebted for this term to the people at Pricewaterhouse Coopers.

Chapter 12

1. For those working with for-profit companies, an easily read, short (138 pages) book on business thinking is Charan, Ram. 2001. *What the CEO Wants You to Know: How Your Company Really Works.* New York: Random House.

2. Interesting work on this subject has been done on the frequency of informal communications among researchers, who, like professionals, can provide more benefits to their companies if they share ideas. See Allen, Thomas J. 1977. *Managing the Flow of Technology.* Cambridge: MIT Press.

Chapter 15

1. Several such cases are described in O'Shea, James and Charles Madigan. 1997. *Dangerous Company: The Consulting Powerhouses and the Business They Save and Ruin.* New York: Times Business Random House.

2. This concern was raised at least as early as 1969. See Higdon, Hal. 1969. *The Business Healers.* New York: Random House, pp. 274–275.

3. Schroeder, Michael. June 20, 2001. "SEC Fines Arthur Andersen in Fraud Case," *Wall Street Journal.*

4. Hines, Crystal Nix. May 31, 2001. "Competition Sprouts One-Stop Law Firms: Diversification Means Higher Profits, But Opens Door to Ethical Concerns," *New York Times,* Section C, page C1.

Index

A

Account managers, 120–23
  account ownership and, 151–52
  as client advocates, 149–50
  client control and, 125–26, 148–49
  earning account introductions
    from, 152–54
  as firm representative, 152
  long-term orientation of, 123
  qualifications of, 121–23
  relationship strength and, 121–22
  team attitude and, 122–23
  wrong, 195–96
  See also Salespeople
Accounts. *See* Clients
Account teams
  account management and, 122–23
  makeup of, 123–24
  management support of, 124–25
  solution sets and, 125–31
Action-orientation, 9, 192
Andersen, Arthur, 87
Archie, Will, 94

B

Benchmarking, 92, 105
Benjamin, Carol, 165–66
BEST management questions,
  114–15

BEST Selling Model, 15–22, 218
  action orientation of, 9, 192
  criteria, 8–10
  defined, 15
  diagram, 16
  evaluation questions, 114–15
  example, 20–22
  exercise, 109–13
  flexibility and, 9
  initial projects and, 16–18
  levers, 117–18
  practicality/simplicity of, 9
  See also Buyers; Events; Signals;
    Techniques
Beverly, Bruce, 13
Borden, Mark, 37
Borsch, Bob, 52, 53
Boudreau, Jeff, 96, 168
Bridge buyers, 18, 51
Bridging techniques, 91, 102–3
Business case techniques, 91, 103–5,
  113
Buskuhl, Joe, xviii, 86
Buyers, 41–54, 109
  bridge, 18, 51
  categories of, 18
  cross-functional, 18, 50–51
  functional, 18, 51–52
  missing, 196–97

Buyers *(continued)*
    proper level of, 52–53
    relationship expansion and, 48–54
    rising star, 53–54
    as sponsors, 48–50
    synergy with, 44–47
    team evaluation of, 114–15
    value of, 41–44

C

Carr, Abby Gouverneur, 86
Caso, Joe, 19, 98
Cawthorne, Gary, 74
Clients
    contacting, 28–29, 155–56,
        171–72, 175–77
    control of, 125–26, 148–49
    ethics and, 26–27, 146–48, 204,
        205–15
    events and, 55–71
    intelligence, 177–78
    interests first, 26–27, 146–48, 204,
        205–15
    internal hostilities, xxvi, 46–47
    introductions to, 152–54
    loyalty, xiv–xvi
    maintaining, xvii–xviii, 3–8, 202–3
    resistance from, xxiv–xxvi
    rules of engaging, 146–56
    spending time with, 56–58, 71
    understanding, 4, 5, 45–47,
        164–66
    See also Relationships
Cohen, Hollace, 54, 98
Communications
    as BEST lever, 118
    best-practices recognition, 174–75
    client knowledge and, 45–47
    confusion elimination with, 157–58
    institutional, 170–78
    internal networking, 159–64

with key decision-makers, 8, 28–29
    mutual update, 155, 169–70,
        175–76
    obstacles, xxiii
    portal project, 25–26, 28–29
    as sales tool, xxiii
    trust-building and, 158–59,
        163–64, 172–74
Compensation
    commission-based, 186–89
    for cooperation, 143
    discretionary, 182–84
    schedule-based, 184–86
    See also Rewards
Consolidation, industry, xvi
Control freaks, xxii
Corey, Jim, 94
Corey, Mike, 41, 51
Cross-functional buyers, 18, 50–51
Cross-selling
    accountability, 203–4
    action orientation of, 9, 192
    adding practices in, xvii
    advantages, xii–xix, xxiv–xxvi
    agenda clarity, 200
    conclusion, 217–18
    defined, 10–14
    ethics, 205–15
    failures, 191–204
    goal alignment, 197–98
    integrated solutions, 12–14, 126–28
    internal networking for, 159–64
    interview questions, 160–61
    kinds of, xviii–xix
    opportunities to pass, 194–95
    reasons for, xi–xxvii
    role adoption, 166–69
    specialization and, xx–xxii
    unrelated needs and, 10, 11
    upstream/downstream, 11–12
    weakest link, 198–99

See also BEST Selling Model;
Buyers; Events; Signals;
Techniques
Cross-selling model. *See* BEST
Selling Model
Customer relationship management
(CRM), 176–77, 178

D

Danholt, Henrik, 106
Davies, Dwight, 25
Decisions, 3, 8, 139
Dunham, Audie, 85

E

Engagement rules. *See* Rules of
engagement
Ethics, 26–27, 205–15
client priorities and, 26–27,
146–48, 204, 209–12
referrals and, 208–9
selling vs. advising, 212–14
Events, 18–19, 55–71, 109
agenda, following, 154–55
celebration, 59, 68
checklist of, 58–60
client education, 59, 67–68
drop-by, 59, 68–69
examples of, 20–22, 112
fact-finding, 58, 60–61
idea/consensus-building, 59, 65–66
negotiating, 59, 66
ownership of, 154
participation rules, 154–55
professional, 60, 70–71
sales, 59, 69
signals at, 85–87
social and service, 60, 69–70
strategizing and planning, 59,
64–65
team evaluation of, 114–15

travel, 59, 66–67
update and review, 59, 62–64

F

Flexibility, 9, 91
Fredericks, Bill, 68
Fritz, David, 79
Functional buyers, 18, 51–52
Functional thinking,
xix–xxii, 157–78

G

Geier, Guy, 49
Growth
in consolidating industry, xvi
in mature markets, xvi–xvii
Gustafson, Bill, 66

H

Harris, David, 48
Heiman, Stephen, 18
Hirth, Bob, 161
Hoeberlein, Wayne, 12
Hoenle, Martin, 66
Hotchkiss, Anita, 70

I

Information source buyers, 18
In-selling, xix, 113
Institutional obstacles, xxii–xxiv

J

Jacoby, Frank, xvii
Jolls, Jack, xxv, 85

K

Kasparek, Ed, 99
Keyko, David, 31, 78, 147
Klein, Gary, 3
Krauss, Bob, xiii, 78, 100

L

Lee, Bill, 37
LoBue, Carl, xv, 73–74
Loyalty, xiv–xvi

M

Macro-signals, 19, 76–81
  disconnects as, 80–81
  executive activity as, 78
  financial strategies as, 81
  job changing as, 79–80
  professional hirings as, 78–79
  work delays/stoppages as, 79
Maggioto, Rocco, 23, 24
Maister, David, xxiv
Manganelli, Ray, 79
Mature markets, xvi–xvii
McKee, Robert, 176
McNaughton, Bruce, 50, 94
Meiland, Dan, 71
Mergers, xvi
Micro-signals, 19, 81–88
  asking for, 88
  client questions as, 85
  events and, 85–87
  staffing to detect, 82–84
  surfacing, 87–88
  training to recognize, 84–85
Miller, Robert, 18
Mistakes, xiv–xv, 3–4, 5
Murnane, Tom, 27, 105

N

Nash, David, 63

O

Obstacles, xix–xxvi, 47
  client resistance, xxiv–xxvi
  functional thinking, xix–xxii
  individual-level, xix–xxii
  institutional-level, xxii–xxiv

O'Hare, Connie, 148
Organizations
  cross-selling confusion in, 157–58
  designing, 140–41
  managing business pipelines, 177
  rules of engagement, 26–27,
    145–56, 204, 205–15
  structures for cooperation, 139–43
  See also Communications;
    Compensation
Osterman, David, 173

P

Palmer, Mike, 56, 88, 102, 104, 204
Pedestal selling, 94–95
Peters, Mike, 69, 214
Phernambucq, Stan, 92
Pidot, Whitney, 173
Ping, David, 81
Pollino, Pat, 158
Portal projects, 23–39
  contacts for, 28–29, 155–56,
    171–72, 175–77
  creating services for, 37–39
  criteria, 26–37
  cutting edge approach of, 35
  defined, 15–16
  ethics and, 26–27, 146–48, 204,
    205–15
  example of, 21
  at functional intersections,
    35–36
  immediacy of need and, 29–31
  non-threatening nature, 32–36
  pricing, 23–25, 27–28
  services to emphasize for, 36–37
  value to client, 31–32
Pratesi, Roger, 80
Presumptive selling, 91, 95–97, 113
Price resistance, 27–28
Prieto, Bob, xvii

Professionals
  adopting cross seller role, 166–69
  arrogance of, 135–38, 148–49,
    175–76
  decision-makers and, 139
  displacing, 201–2
  functional thinking and, xix–xxii,
    157–78
  organization structure and, 140–41
  recruiting, 141
  salespeople vs., 133–43
  sales skills and, xxii, 137–39
  specialization and, xx–xxii
  tendencies of, 135–38
  trust-building and, 158–59,
    163–64, 172–74
  understanding clients, 4, 5, 45–47,
    164–66
Profit, xiii–xiv

Q

Questioning techniques, 91, 97–99
Quinn, Stephen, 67, 147

R

Referrals, 208–9
Relationships, 41
  account management and, 3–8,
    121–22
  bridges, 18, 51
  clients' internal, xxvi, 46–47
  earning introductions in, 152–54
  enemies, 202–3
  ethics and, 26–27, 146–48, 204,
    205–15
  events and, 55–71
  expansion of, 48–54
  internal, 159–64, 192–93
  investing time in, 56–58, 71
  lost, 200–201
  ownership of, 151
  power of many, 45, 55–56, 75,
    119–20
  synergy of, 44–47
  See also Clients
Relationship starters. *See* Portal
  projects
Resource allocation, 117–18, 119–31
  account management, 120–23
  account team, 123–25
  as BEST lever, 117–18
  solution set, 125–31
Rewards, 179–89
  as BEST levers, 118
  as obstacles, xxiii–xxiv
  personal, xviii
  promotions as, xviii
  system challenges, 179–82
  See also Compensation
Robinette, Muriel, 82, 84, 101
Rules of engagement, 145–56
  account introduction, 152–54
  account manager roles, 149–50, 152
  account ownership, 151–52
  client control, 148–49
  client interests first, 26–27,
    146–48, 204, 205–15
  contacts, 28–29, 155–56, 171–72,
    175–77
  event participation, 154–55
  firm representation, 152
  mutual update, 155
  relationship ownership, 151
  selling vs. doing, 149
Ruotolo, Frank, 46

S

Salespeople
  arrogance of, 135–38
  decision-makers and, 139
  integrating, 139–43
  organization structure and, 139–43

Salespeople *(continued)*
  professionals vs., 133–43
  recruiting, 141
  tendencies of, 135–38
  trust-building and, 158–59,
    163–64, 172–74
  understanding clients, 4, 5, 45–47,
    164–66
Sales skills
  account management and,
    xxii–xxiii
  professionals and, xxii, 137–39
Seeding ideas, 91, 99–102
Service quality, xv
Seymour, Barry, 20
Sher, Beth, 31, 92, 93
Sherman, Les, 55, 56, 57
Shine, William, 164
Signals, 19, 73–88, 109, 112
  defined, 73
  at events, 85–87
  hearing, 75
  public vs. personal, 73–75, 76–77
  sources of, 73–76
  surfacing, 87–88
  team evaluation of, 114–15
  See also Macro-signals;
    Micro-signals
Smith, Milton, 89, 90
Solution sets, 125–31
  defined, 125
  integrated vs. seamless, 126–28
  issues/champions identification, 130
  materials development, 130–31
  matrix, 128–29
  sample, 128
  task force selection, 130
  vision-selling and, 126–28
Specialization as obstacle, xx–xxii
Sponsors, 48–50, 91, 92–94, 113
Stern, Milton, xiii

Sullivan, Dennis, 48, 51, 100

T

Teams. *See* Account teams
Techniques, 19, 89–107, 109, 112–13
  benchmarking, 92, 105
  bridging, 91, 102–3
  business case, 91, 103–5, 113
  checklist of, 91–92
  examples of, 21, 112–13
  pedestal selling, 91, 94–95
  presumptive selling, 91, 95–97, 113
  questioning, 91, 97–99, 113
  seeding ideas, 91, 99–102
  sponsorship request, 91, 92–94, 113
  team evaluation of, 115
  vision-selling, 92, 106–7, 113,
    126–28
Tindale, Bruce, 153
Trial engagements. *See* Portal projects
Trust-building, 158–59, 163–64,
  172–74

V

Value, xiii, 8, 27, 31–32, 196–97,
  214–15
Vernon, Steve, 57, 96–97, 98, 207
Vision-selling techniques, 92, 106–7,
  113, 126–28

W

Wedges. *See* Portal projects
Weitzel, Mark, 36, 67, 103
Weyl, Alan, 45, 104
Wilson, Ian B., 13

Y

Youssef, Emad, 10–11